Go Ahead!

Unleash a Contagious
Customer Success Culture

Also by Barry S. Farah

Customer Success, 1998

The Magic Wand, 2017

Go Ahead!

Unleash a Contagious
Customer Success Culture

Barry S. Farah

authorHOUSE®

AuthorHouse™
1663 Liberty Drive
Bloomington, IN 47403
www.authorhouse.com
Phone: 1 (800) 839-8640

Published by AuthorHouse 05/15/2019

ISBN: 978-1-7283-1197-5 (sc)
ISBN: 978-1-7283-1196-8 (hc)
ISBN: 978-1-7283-1195-1 (e)

Print information available on the last page.

Customer Success is a trademark of Barry Farah
The Magic Wand is a trademark of Barry Farah
Go Ahead! is a trademark of Barry Farah

Titles by Barry Farah may be purchased for business or promotional use or for special sales. For more information please write to:
Special Markets Department
Baron Books
1880 Office Club Pointe
Colorado Springs, CO 80920

This book is printed on acid-free paper.

Dedication

To my son, David, and my daughter, Alli. As young adults they have both caught the vision of the customer success mindset. In their respective young careers, they have earned accolades from their superiors. They are differentiating themselves by adding value with entrepreneurial energy. They both make me very proud. And, I love 'em.

Acknowledgments

I am grateful to the hundreds of wonderful people I have had the honor to work with over the years . . . a great customer success team!

Special thanks to Randy Welsch and Scott Roehr, who really embody the customer success mindset. They are successful in their own business endeavors, but previously I had the honor of working with them. Randy was president of Master Solutions, LLC (MSL) and Scott was COO of The Personnel Department, Inc. before I sold those companies. They provided excellent suggestions for this book, but more importantly they live it.

And, to John Bolin, a fantastic guy – creative, smart and a lot of fun. He gets customer success and helped with the title. And, to the copyeditor, Tia Smith—she is great.

And to Tracy Lyn of Virtually Possible Designs. How did she hit a winner like you see on the cover? By being very customer success minded. Great job Tracy!

Table of Contents

Introduction   1

Part One: A Foundation for Customer Success

Chapter 1: Beyond Customer Service   7

Chapter 2: Helping Your Customers Succeed   17

Chapter 3: Principle-Based Business   41

Chapter 4: Retaining the Right Customers   55

Part Two: A Customer Success Mindset

Chapter 5: Hiring Go Ahead! People   71

Chapter 6: Customer Success Culture   79

Chapter 7: Cohesion Starts at the Top   93

Part Three: The Customer Success Way

Chapter 8: Getting Customers the Right Way   107

Chapter 9: Customer Success Training   117

Chapter 10: Keeping the Momentum   133

Appendixes

Appendix A: The Five Secrets of Exceptional CX   141

Appendix B: Sales and Negotiations IBM Sales Approach   143

Appendix C: Otto's Auto Repair Shop   149

Appendix D: Integrity, Innovation, and Invitation   153

Appendix E: Behaviors of a Salesperson   157

Appendix F: New Hire Orientation   159

Introduction

The objective of this book is to provide the framework to unleash a contagious customer success culture. Customer success is a mindset. Mine developed from years of observation and passion. Throughout my life, I've started and run several companies. Some have been more successful than others, but I'm an entrepreneur at my core and love to add value for the customer.

It seems like I have always had customers. In elementary school, I sold Christmas cards and flashlights door to door. In junior high, I squeezed my own lawn care business in between soccer games. In high school, I owned a profitable landscaping business and sold siding, vacuum cleaners, water treatment equipment, and steel buildings. During college, I owned a tree-trimming, landscaping, and remodeling business.

By the time I obtained my undergraduate degree at twenty-one, it seemed I had experienced a business career, but I had much more to learn. After a two-year stint at IBM, I earned an MBA, worked for Ford Motor Company, and then joined the Strategic Consulting division of Crowe Chizek. These experiences taught me people management, disciplined my problem-solving skills, and strengthened my financial analytics and my strategic planning ability. I was on the fast track but realized that, for me, striking out on my own was the better path. So I did.

In 1991, at twenty-eight, I built my first company as an adult—The Personnel Department, Inc.—and ran it for more than twenty years. Concurrently, at thirty-four, I built a satellite and radar systems business and ran it for twelve years. Our guys were the architects on a complex upgrade of satellite and radar systems—some likened it to swapping out a jet engine while in flight. In 2010, I sold that company to the developers of NASA's Hubble Telescope program.

In my thirties, I realized my greatest satisfaction as an entrepreneur was more than making a profit; it was the joy of helping others succeed. I was profit-motivated, but I wanted a corporate culture that was bigger than money.

I wanted to create an environment where everyone could grow, and where we helped our customers in exceptional ways. I wanted a company that was bursting with energy and highly respected.

We experienced some success. I expanded my company into a full suite of business services in forty-three states and three countries at its peak before I started selling the business to four different buyers over a ten-year period.

I launched into commercial developments in Colorado, California, and North Dakota. Things were going well until I decided to build a large hotel in Minot, North Dakota, when the price of oil was at its peak. We opened the doors on time—but oil plummeted from $110 a barrel to $26. And occupancy followed the price of oil. I got my butt kicked.

I jumped back into technology in 2014 with a Capital Partner. I acquired four technology companies; put my cultural stamp of Integrity, Innovation, and Invitation upon them; served as CEO; and, at the time of this writing, just closed on selling my stake back to the Capital Partner.

At the core of my personal purpose, I enjoy creating an exceptional culture that opens the door for others to achieve great things. What I've discovered and implemented along the way is a customer success philosophy that makes business more fun because it is based on values and principles first.

In 1998, I wrote my first book on customer success. I'm told that I coined the term. In 2017, I wrote *The Magic Wand*, describing in story form the five steps to deliver an exceptional customer experience. In this book, I'll distinguish customer success from customer service; describe how to build a customer success culture, hire the right people, and sell with integrity; and propose a plan to sustain it. I argue that customer success protects you from being a casualty of disruption.

The roots of disruption are within. We often constrain ourselves from offering a great customer experience. In this book, I argue that setting people free to break the rules— giving them the authority to solve the customer's actual problem—will equip you to gradually disrupt yourself before you are a casualty of a nimble competitor.

Go Ahead!—set your people free to lead their domain, to be proactive, to deliver what your customers really want before they ask. Unleash the positive peer pressure that comes from a customer success culture. It is not based on rules—it is a mindset, and it is contagious. People prefer an uplifting, energetic, problem-solving culture. It is a lot of fun.

I hope these principles are helpful to you.

Part One: A Foundation for Customer Success

Chapter 1: Beyond Customer Service

"Get closer than ever to your customers. So close, in fact, that you tell them what they need well before they realize it themselves." —Steve Jobs

Sears, Roebuck and Company sold everything from hubcaps to house kits, had a great company culture, and minted millionaire retirees way before Silicon Valley. With their vast resources, ever wonder why they didn't become Google or Amazon or Walmart?

In their glory days, Sears diligently reinvented themselves around the customer, and in many ways, they defined a customer success mindset. So, what happened? They always tried to have good customer service. They even put a coat on a chair in the conference room to remind them to think about the customer. But it was just a coat—not an actual customer. How did such smart people miss what the market demanded by such a big gap?

Previous employees, including CEOs, and customers have publicly cited Sears's key mistakes: they shouldn't have purchased the troubled retailer, Kmart; they shouldn't have purchased a "never discount the price" retailer, Lands' End; they shouldn't have spun off a destination brand like Craftsman. In other words, they should have stuck to their knitting.

Sears should have listened to their middle-income customers and not diversified into financial services. Or, at a minimum, they should not have taken their eye off the ball and allowed that diversification to distract them—they were the king of the retail hill in the '70s. They should have dug deeper into what a *new* retail would look like. If they had focused their expertise on cracking *the hard* at that time, they would not have dismissed Walmart, The Home Depot, Best Buy, and Target. Sears was the largest retailer until 1989, but they should have made substantial adjustments to new stores in the early '80s before it was too late.

That rings true, but evidence of the systemic shift commenced in the late '70s and culminated in 1993. At this time the CEO's aggregated belief was that he had to either fix the stores or fix the catalog business. This false choice could have been avoided by deploying some customer success tools. Rather, they abandoned their catalog business for pragmatic reasons: 50,000 employees and a cost structure that was not sustainable.

What Sears had was a gold mine of customer experience strategy and service delivery that just needed updating. They had data on every inventory item and every customer's preferences. And they enjoyed sole ownership of this data on so many millions of customers. More importantly, the catalog business was the emotional connection between the customer and the company. It was the foundation of their customers' loyalty.

Would a customer success mindset really have helped? Customer *success* argues for a principled foundation to focus proactively on the customer. Sometimes, we make business too complicated. Very capable, good people with good intentions missed the need for a deep customer connection.

What needed to happen was a roll-up-your-sleeves approach to deepening that customer loyalty. If we need to replace the catalog with something equally or more informative that is less expensive to produce and distribute, what form would that take to maintain or even improve the emotional customer connection? We certainly can't leave the customer in the lurch and yank away their connection to us.

In the early '90s, email was already prevalent in the business community—and the trend for everyday households was unmistakable. By 1996, 10 percent of Americans were users, meaning almost everyone was only two degrees away from a user. Just a few years later, in 2001, 50 percent of Americans were users. Sears had an early adopter approach to the internet in the late '90s. So, the error was not a lack of sophistication.

The wrong questions were asked. They were looking at the catalog business through the lens of what it cost to deliver. They had forgotten that the real value of Sears was the story built around all their products. It wasn't the products themselves; it was the fact that they made the customer feel thought of all the time. From jeans for your school-aged kids that never wore out to fashionable women's suits blazing the trail in the '70s to tools that fixed things around the house—inspired. Everything had a purpose—they were thinking like the customer and offering solutions, like back in 1908 when they introduced a home kit that would be delivered near your plot of land via railroad. "Those guys up there at Sears sure seem to know what I'm thinking before I do—but now that you mention it, that is exactly what I want."

The questions that should have been asked were, "Before we drop the catalog and fix the stores, how can we make the customer more successful? How can we return to the place where the customer sees us as the proactive problem-solver of all their household needs? What would make her reconnect with us?" Then the capable executive team could have uncovered the value of what they had right in front of them. They had customer data and all the accompanying predictive analytics, but it was lying latent. What built the company was the catalog, and they abandoned it.

By starting from a platform of proactively helping the customer succeed, they would not have allowed themselves to forsake the source of their customers' loyalty. This approach to business demonstrates how the customer success mindset can bring clarity in the middle of the business fog.

"This approach to business demonstrates how the customer success mindset can bring clarity in the middle of the business fog."

They could have identified that a phased digital replacement would make sense. They could have laid down the gauntlet: we will not yank the story of our connection with the customer (the Sears catalog) away from them until we figure out a suitable replacement. Perhaps, in 1993 and 1994, Sears could have requested by snail mail that all those catalog customers send in their email addresses for special offers that would emerge before the next catalog was issued. They would have had the largest email database in the world at the time. And they could have started sending components of the catalog by email until things developed further. Perhaps they could have purchased AOL or one of the smaller providers that no one remembers from back in 1992 and built on the story of deepened loyalty for everything from hubcaps to home kits—giving them ownership and direct access to this *new internet thing*.

Since hindsight is so much easier than being on the field of play at the time, this review may seem a bit unfair. I wish Sears the best in their endeavor to recover from bankruptcy. Still, they would not have dumped their customers' loyalty without a replacement if they had implemented a customer success mindset.

Customer success mitigates against market disruption. It is proactive. So, in the example above, dating back to the

11

late '70s, a customer success mindset would have provided actionable market intelligence from its customers. And if that intelligence had been acted upon, Sears would be equal to or greater than Walmart, Amazon, or Google today.

"Customer success mitigates against market disruption."

Customer *service* actually requires more work than customer *success*. The success of a customer service program depends almost entirely on the management team's ability to convey and enforce the rules. Customer *success* requires leadership, but since the motivation is internalized with a transcendent vision, it manages itself.

In some situations, the outward behavior of a customer *success* representative would vary only slightly from that of a customer *service* representative. However, what is transpiring inside the employee's mind is radically different. He has an internal compass that benefits the customer. He delivers the service with a purpose, and that purpose is broader than a set of rules.

Customer *service* is reactionary by nature, and business leaders usually treat it as an element of business that requires continuous behavioral training. And external training is tedious. Customer *success*, on the other hand, establishes a higher standard. When properly adopted by your employees, it resonates with your customers and motivates them to reward you with the best kind of loyalty—the kind that translates into repeat business and referrals. As the leaders and employees embrace the mindset, it is like an avalanche careening down a mountain. It builds its own momentum, creating excitement in your customers and your employees.

Customer *service* often tends to be superficial and responsive. Customer *success* argues for a proactive, more meaningful alternative. It provides the tools necessary to equip an employee mindset that motivates innovative and diligent problem-solving on behalf of the customer.

Customer success is enterprising, bold, and dynamic. It fosters ingenuity and inventiveness. The customer success employee is personally in control of his work. As a result, the customer success representative is more than an employee. He is a partner-in-training. He is filled with purpose. By definition, he is bounding with initiative and energy.

Customer success representatives are more ambitious, more resourceful, and have more fun than the typical customer service employee. Here's why: the customer success discipline helps foster an environment that celebrates the truly innovative. These employees are not waiting for a flash of brilliance. They are simply *determined* to create and develop new services or products that meet their customer's needs.

"These employees are not waiting for a flash of brilliance. They are simply determined to create and develop new services or products that meet their customer's needs."

Customer success does not require profound intelligence or even a lot of extra time. It does demand active leadership. It results in a powerful, energizing, and fun corporate culture that can captivate the loyalty of your customers.

A customer success mindset will help you approach your customers with new vigor. It ultimately argues on behalf of releasing the creative inventor inside of each employee. Every payroll processor, benefits administrator, auto mechanic, carpenter, marketing manager, retail attendant, accountant, and executive possesses an untapped creative component that wants to help people solve their problems. Our job is to fan the flames of this powerful drive and unleash it.

***

Here are some of the primary differences between a customer success and customer service environment:

Customer Success	Customer Service
Asks open-ended questions	Asks discrete questions
Fueled by purpose	Directed by rules
Authority to solve problems	Higher authority required
Proactive	Reactive
Fun	Difficult
Inventive	Prescriptive

Chapter 2: Helping Your Customers Succeed

"Just having satisfied customers isn't good enough anymore. If you really want a booming business, you have to create raving fans." —Ken Blanchard

Often little companies grow more rapidly than big ones, in spite of their distinct limitations. The little company is often undercapitalized, possesses fewer training and development resources, and is limited on executive and managerial talent. Yet the likes of little Uber at the time beat the much larger Yellow Cab. The upstart Away provides sleek, lightweight, durable luggage that charges your devices at the same time. The luggage business in 2016 was a crowded industry, yet Away outflanked the bigger competition. In some cases, the smaller guy sets up shop right next door and erodes the big guy's market share right out from under his nose.

What is happening with this phenomenon? The little guy brings to the market something no one else is thinking about: innovative ways that enable customers to succeed.

Customer success requires action. It does not wait for problems. It proactively fixes them before they arise. There are seven components that define this passion to help a customer succeed.

"Customer success requires action. It does not wait for problems. It fixes them before they arise."

1. Discover the customer's values and history.

Customer success invests more time during the initial stages of a customer relationship. It will *Go Ahead* and invest in customer orientation. One of the first questions my employees ask a new client is why they purchased our service. Why did they buy from us instead of the competition? This provides insight into how we can serve the customer according to his priorities.

Customer service simply responds to its knowledge of the present situation. If selling to businesses, customer success wants to learn about the company's values, the technology it employs, how long the company has been in business, and so forth. Customer success will understand the ownership structure as well as the corporate philosophy, mission, vision, and values. It will discover how many people the business employs and its plans for the future. Customer success will find the level to which the company has accomplished its goals in the past, particularly as it relates to the service or product provided. It will also explore the expectations for this business relationship.

Customer success will ask, "What would we need to do to cause the use of our services to be one of the best business decisions you have made? How would that differ from the last vendor's performance?"

In retail, customer success will seek to understand more than the customer's demographics and preferences. An example is in the highly competitive hospitality industry. A customer success agent will tailor-make a reservation to suit the customer's need.

Customer service would be satisfied with a general profile: the customer prefers four-star accommodations, a nonsmoking room with a king-size bed and a rollaway for the munchkin. Customer success would ask more questions: "What was your favorite vacation? Describe the food, entertainment, and accommodations. What kind of memories would you like to build while you are on your next vacation? Are you interested in a restful or lively experience?"

Customer success will have a general grasp of the major disappointments the customer has experienced. It will have asked enough open-ended questions to be equipped to proactively make the customer's experience exceptional. Customer success focuses on the customer's values and preferences. Customer success does not try to fashion the customer into its description of what is fun, pleasant, or smart business. It will help the customer uncover his own.

Knowing the customer's values and history is really about knowing his story.

"Customer success will have asked enough open-ended questions to be equipped to proactively make the customer's experience exceptional."

2. Anticipate the customer's real needs.

Customer service handles questions and issues when the customer calls. That's nice, but it is much better to anticipate the problem before she calls. Customer success will *Go Ahead* and anticipate the customer's need before it arises.

It's not hard to beat the customer to the punch because she has so much on her mind. The customer is not thinking about your company for a service-related issue until the problem is severe enough for her to interrupt her day to call you. Thinking about the customer—even when the customer is not thinking of you—puts the customer success team in a proactive posture. You are ready for anything.

The customer does not have the level of expertise you have in your product line or area of service. You are the expert, and so only you know all the benefits of what you can provide. Realistically, how can this be done? Here's an example.

One of our companies served small companies with fewer than two hundred employees. Most of these businesses were privately held and run by an entrepreneur, who typically had a family member handling bookkeeping and payroll. One of the services our company provided was payroll administration. And direct deposit was less of a thing in the '90s.

When Thanksgiving rolled around, most entrepreneurs were not thinking about payroll logistics. Even the person responsible for providing us with the payroll inputs was too busy to consider that the inputs needed to be submitted early if the employees were to receive their checks on Wednesday instead of Friday, the most common pay date.

One of our employees would call the week before and say, "I know you usually provide us with payroll inputs on Monday, but if I could get those from you earlier, you won't have to worry about it next week and I'll have the payroll checks ready for you before you take off for Thanksgiving."

The customer said, "Oh my gosh, is it already Thanksgiving? I thought we were still in October. Great idea. I'm glad you called."

Taking this extra two minutes in advance saved them and us hours of time trying to fix a problem later. The alternative would be to provide a lot of reactionary customer service during the week of Thanksgiving.

A customer service environment responds to the customer's verbalized needs. Customer success goes beyond this and proactively assesses what the customer *really* needs to succeed. When you think about what the customer *might need* based on what you know, you can reduce the amount of unplanned service you have to provide. I am not suggesting that you can always be calling your customers in advance of them calling you; I am simply suggesting that you think about it.

If you give *thought* to preempting the customer, you will rarely be caught off guard when she does call. This includes delving into the needs that the customer may not be aware of. Even if the customer initiates the inquiry or registers a complaint, the customer success representative will be better equipped to turn the call into a productive and meaningful discussion. He has a better chance of having thought through the customer's inquiry before she calls. Through experience and forethought, the representative understands what the customer will need and is ready for most of the challenges that he will encounter.

How does this work in an ice cream shop? Let's say the primary problem is service delivery speed. Improve delivery speed with layout redesign and attentiveness training and utilize technology to assess when there is likely to be a burst in demand, such as after a ball game. Plan and schedule for that, and the customer will be impressed by your preparation.

The customer success representative allocates energy and thought toward identifying the genuine needs of the customer before the customer tweets, texts, emails, calls, or shows up. When the customer calls, the representative can confidently and swiftly address the need of the moment, because he has already thought about the problem of the hour.

"The customer success representative allocates energy and thought toward identifying the genuine needs of the customer before the customer tweets, texts, emails, calls, or shows up."

3. Resolve the customer's symptoms and address the root cause.

Customer service is primarily defensive. The customer calls with a problem, and the representative is on the run. He may handle the issue at hand with composure, but often he just sits there waiting for the next question. The customer success representative avoids "reaction mode." He answers the question, but quickly turns toward deeper issues.

Where customer service may put a Band-Aid on the wound, customer success will first clean it out. Customer success looks for the right opportunity to go to the next level. It is thinking, "What caused this problem in the first place?" Customer success is looking for the real culprit, while still solving the problem on the surface that the customer presented. The representative is really the project leader, properly provoking the customer to help drive the process and uncover the best and most correct solution. The customer becomes a participant in a productive problem-solving endeavor.

"Where customer service may put a Band-Aid on the wound, customer success will first clean it out."

23

In the customer success environment, the representative is mostly on offense. It starts out with a defensive play, responding to the customer's inquiry, but it quickly moves to a productive attack on the source of the problem. Armed with authority, he will go ahead and fix the underlying problem.

This flies in the face of methodology at some help desks. After you finally get through the phone tree, which screams, "We don't want to talk to you in person," the major performance criterion seems to be, "What is it going to take to get you to give me a good review?" Time is money, but we are talking about the customer's time, not ours. A customer service representative may get the customer off the phone feeling a little better, but the business isn't fixed. Another customer will need to call on that same issue again. In the long term, the customer spends less time with a customer success representative.

Customer service focuses on *answering* questions and appeasing the customer but may miss the point. Customer success will *Go Ahead* and focus on *asking* questions and is bent on uncovering the source of the distress.

"Customer service focuses on *answering* questions and appeasing the customer but may miss the point. Customer success will Go Ahead and focus on *asking* questions and is bent on uncovering the source of the distress."

4. Go beyond what is customary—do a backflip.

We authorize our team to do a backflip. What we mean is that armed with a customer success bias, they have permission to do something out of the ordinary for the benefit of the customer. For example, one of our customer success representatives was hit with a service emergency late on a Friday afternoon. She was the only employee in the office. The customer, in a distant city, had not received their payroll checks, which normally would have arrived by noon. These employees were suspicious of direct deposit and continued to receive "live" checks even in the 2010s. The customer's employees were a finicky group and in a matter of hours had become irate. The overnight shipper had failed. The checks were somewhere between Indianapolis and Atlanta.

Our customer success representative knew the customer's employees were essential and very difficult to replace. So, she did a backflip. She wired money directly into each of the seventeen employees' bank accounts. For those without bank accounts, she had cash delivered to their home. She never mentioned that it was not our "fault." She followed up with cards to each of the customer's employees and sent flowers and a box of chocolates to the customer. This was an expensive solution—but we had previously given authority to the customer success representative to make decisions like this based on her judgment and overall knowledge of the customer.

25

An adequate solution would have been to allow the customer to receive their paychecks on the next business day. After all, it wasn't our fault and it was very close to the wire cutoff time. Mediocre solutions are often satisfactory to the customer service representative. They seem to look at the clock for an excuse. If we shifted blame, we would have lost the customer.

But, our customer success representative was trained to perform a simple calculation in her head. Does the investment in solving the problem have a likely positive return? The cost or investment to perform the backflip was $300. She simply asked herself, "Would I invest $300 plus the cost of my time and effort to keep a customer with an annual profit of many times the investment?"

The boundary-free mentality does not require an emergency to show off. It *probes* for an even better solution to the customer's problem. Though this requires more energy, it really doesn't take a lot more time. It uses the problem-solving schematic detailed in chapter 8.

Often customer service representatives get so caught up in the quagmire of the problem that *relief* is the only positive emotion they feel when they get the customer off the phone. Short term, that may make sense, but it is not customer success.

"Often customer service representatives get so caught up in the quagmire of the problem that relief is the only positive emotion they feel when they get the customer off the phone."

The customer success representative understands capital allocation. I don't mean in terms of a sophisticated merger or acquisition, but he does understand the return on taking a few more minutes or investing a few more dollars to provide a potent solution that saves a customer or deepens customer loyalty.

5. Lead the customer.

Customer success guides the customer. When you lead the customer, you provide him with a more thorough and complete solution. Google, Amazon, and Apple provided the customer with what they wanted long before the customer had any idea what the product or service would do for them.

We encourage our team to *Go Ahead* and become the expert on what the customer needs before he knows he needs it. Then lead him down the best path. Reorganize service delivery offerings in ways that are relevant to the success of the customer. Develop a list of questions that help the customer discover what he really wants.

"Reorganize your service offerings in ways that are relevant to the success of your customer."

Consider a server in a three-star restaurant. "What'll ya have?" is customer service. A customer success server would ask tactful questions about what kind of dining *experience* you would prefer. She would be well versed on the menu and proper combinations. When the customer

27

asks, "What's good here?" she would not say, "Everything, hon', kinda depends on what ya want." That puts it back in the customer's lap. Customer success never prematurely puts responsibility back into the hands of the customer. It also doesn't impose the personal preferences of the server on the customer. It would never say, "Well, I really like the chicken fried steak because I can't resist cream gravy."

Customer success is much more helpful. The server is not leaning on the table, but courteously offers decision-making help. "Tonight, we are offering three types of dining experiences though our menu reflects fifteen entrée choices. Are you in the mood for a spicy hot plate, a full-bodied dish, or a rich and creamy taste for your main entrée?" The leading questions help the customer narrow things down. If the customer chooses spicy, then the server could *lead* the customer through the five entrées that are spicy. She would not say, "We have fish, pork, and chicken. What'll it be?" She is leading with knowledge-based questions, and her expert guidance helps you decide precisely what kind of dining experience you want. And you thought she was just a server!

You might be thinking, *You can't be serious. Do you know how long it would take to train a server in this manner, not to mention the time it takes to delve into the specific interests of the customers at each table?*

First, training your people on product knowledge is critical to enlarging their job. The server is not just a server. She is in charge of engineering successful dining experiences.

She has the authority and the responsibility to improve customer loyalty. She now feels respected by her boss and believes you think she is smart and competent. And that is how she will behave. The reduced recruiting and retention costs far outweigh the cost of training. And training allows you to enlarge the job toward increasing profit.

Second, her thoughtful guidance may take a bit more thought on the front end, but since it is purposeful, it is not wasted. Look around the next time you go to a restaurant. The server can spend a lot of time at each table trying to get the order because she is *answering questions.* And she thinks she will get the best tip by investing her time with chitchat that is relational. But, that makes it about her, not the customer.

Third, it is not more time consuming. Why is she answering questions? So the customer can figure out what he wants! And though relationship building is important, she could unwittingly waste time hobbling between unproductive issues and not asserting with expertise because she isn't trained on how to make more money by asking smart questions.

Finally, during the meal, the chance of a customer sending back a reject dish because "it was not what they expected" is dramatically reduced. By allocating decisive energy on the front end, the server will spend less time replacing food over the course of the meal. And, that leads to a more enjoyable experience.

The issue is simple. It is not about the server or the representative; it is about the customer. They sort of know their preferences. But they are not experts in your product or service. They need to be thoughtfully led.

Here's one more example in the HR consulting business. When your customer calls and says, "I want to fire Billy," customer service might just say, "OK, we can help you fire Billy." Customer success would drive the solution based on expertise. "You know what? We understand your desire to fire Billy on the spot. But we would like to ensure we do this right. To help mitigate against the possibility of a wrongful discharge lawsuit, can I ask you a couple of questions?" One of my previous businesses had four pages of them. Those questions make sure that if the customer is going to fire Billy, the customer is protected.

You don't just want to protect him from being sued. You want to ensure that the remainder of the employees respect him after the employee's tenure with the company is terminated. By guiding the customer, you serve him better and help him become more successful.

Customer service answers questions. It responds and reacts and hopes for a conclusion. Customer success will *Go Ahead* and take the lead, thoughtfully asking questions to guide the customer to an exceptional experience.

"*Customer service answers questions. Customer success takes the lead, thoughtfully asking*

GO AHEAD! – Unleash a Contagious Customer Success Culture

questions to lead the customer to an exceptional service experience."

6. Respond quickly and with agility.

Speed is a critical element of the customer success environment. This ironically starts with as much "old school" interface as possible, augmented by technology. For example, make it easy for the customer to reach you. I understand the financial arguments for having automated voice response, but you are missing out on uncovering a potentially systemic business problem by keeping your customers at bay. Forcing your customers through a complex phone maze forces them to be good to you. If you want to be good to them, make it easy for them to get a problem resolved quickly.

Speed does not mean rushing the customer. It means rushing to serve the customer. It means returning the call when you promised—or sooner—and always opting for now, rather than later, to address an issue.

The concept of speed gives your customer success representatives authority and responsibility to quickly make changes in the business process to kill corporate bottlenecks. Just *Go Ahead* and fix them!

"Speed does not mean rushing the customer. It means rushing to serve the customer."

31

In the olden days, you could manage a business to cash—that is, to make most business decisions around the balance sheet and free cash flows. Then the experts told us we needed to manage our business to share—that is, to gain market share. Though these business methodologies are essential, they are not enough. We need to manage our businesses to time. Speed honors this reality. We can't wait until we lose customers to respond. We need to fix our service delivery system fast.

> **"We need to manage our businesses to time. Speed honors this reality. We can't wait until we lose customers to respond. We need to fix our service delivery system fast."**

The primary reason our companies are not nimble is because we aren't encouraging employees to start from a position of "owning" the customer and rewarding them for "breaking the rules." When we grant freedom inside rational parameters, employees are free to explore—and even make mistakes. We give them permission to *Go Ahead*!

Agility produces solutions that anticipate and overcome customer obstacles. A huge frustration for a customer is to be told by one representative of the company that he can't handle the customer's issue. The customer does not want the service desk to inform him that he must call another department. *"Wait a minute!"* he says to himself. *"I thought I called customer service. Why aren't they handling this for me?"* Do you want to know why? The representative does not want to be put on hold while waiting for that other department to answer either. This is a problem that can come back and bite you.

Agility fixes corporate bottlenecks by requiring employees to face internal frustrations on behalf of the customer. Customer success will never be satisfied with giving a customer a phone number to another department just to get that customer off his plate.

"Agility fixes corporate bottlenecks by requiring employees to face internal frustrations on behalf of the customer."

The customer success representative will call the other office for the customer, find the right person to talk to, and patch the customer through—or even solve the problem offline and call the customer back. This engaged process helps the representative learn how hard it is to be a customer. And after he solves the customer's immediate concern, he will elevate the issue and help fix the internal bottleneck.

"This engaged process helps the representative learn how hard it is to be a customer. And after he solves the customer's immediate concern, he will elevate the issue and help fix the internal bottleneck."

An obstacle is whatever gets in the way of your customer achieving a goal or rational expectation. A customer success environment requires maneuvering around difficulties on behalf of the customer. The agile representative would never frustrate the customer by making him wind through the maze of corporate bureaucracy.

7. Exude a humble posture and remain diligent.

Customer success is also humble. It does not arrogantly believe that it has all the answers. It has an accurate estimation of itself. Customer success is more interested in fixing the problem than placing blame. The customer success representative will take a personal hit and even lose face if it makes the customer better off in the end.

Looking back at the waitress, a customer success–minded server will never intrude upon the dining experience with her personal preferences—it is not about her. It is never perched on top of the world looking down at the customer. Customer success truly listens with the purpose of a real dialogue. It is humble enough to respect and honor and solicit the insights and the wisdom that are hidden in the heart of the customer.

"Customer success truly listens with the purpose of a real dialogue. It is humble enough to respect and honor and solicit the insights and the wisdom that are hidden in the heart of the customer."

This humble approach to serving the customer encourages diligence. It does not assume that an easy answer is on the ready. It is grounded in perseverance. Grit is culturally applauded at the customer success business. A customer success representative will not give up until he gets to the bottom of the real problem and renders the best solution. He will *Go Ahead* and finish.

On the other hand, customer service is usually satisfied when the customer is content—or at least off the phone!

"Grit is culturally applauded at the customer success business. A customer success representative will not give up until he gets to the bottom of the real problem and renders the best solution."

Recreational hiking illustrates this well. In Colorado, we have more than fifty mountains that exceed 14,000 feet. Many of those peaks have trails that an amateur can hike. Often a novice climber will quit before reaching the summit of one of these majestic peaks. I find it interesting that most of those people stop at around 13,000 feet. They get tired of being faked out by the "false summits" (those places that look like the top as you are climbing but are really just a rise in elevation that blocks your view of the real peak). With a little more effort—one last push—they could reach the top and enjoy a 360-degree, 100-mile view.

I find many customer service representatives to be similar. They weaken quickly. They are satisfied with an adequate solution. They often do not persevere. They aren't bad people. They just have not been trained to be energetically and purposefully more proactive.

You don't measure a customer success environment by how many customers are content and, therefore, not bothering you. Rather, you assess it by the degree to which a customer's business or life is better as a result of your service or product delivery. You will know this is happening when you create a real-time dialogue with the customer. And, that is rewarded with loyalty.

The cost of customer success

You might be thinking that the customer success environment is too much work. Is it really worth it to shift from a customer service mindset to a customer success mindset?

Remember the last time you were treated poorly at a department store? Recently, a customer service representative leaned across the counter and looked at me with a lazy glare that almost dared me to go to a competitor. He didn't want to engage in the *exercise of thinking* to solve my problem. After a limited effort, he said, "That's all I can do."

I tried to reason with him, even attempted to do the thinking for him. I wanted to leave the store and try out a competitor, but it was too inconvenient. So, *I* did a backflip to get *him* to help me! My efforts with this customer service representative were in vain. The lights were on, but no one was home.

As I contemplated his behavior, I was struck by how easy it would have been to keep me as a customer if he had just possessed the right mindset. Certainly, he had been trained in his company's nationally respected customer service program. I saw it on his face and felt it in the air. He didn't just forget the duties of customer service—he never got the big idea of customer success.

That day a famous department store lost a good customer, and they will probably never know why. Customer service did not cut the mustard.

The cost of replacing a good customer includes the marketing replacement cost, the operational disruption, and the enormous toll on corporate goodwill.

But what about the cost of missing an entirely new market? Sears missed an opportunity to control the digital catalog business. They didn't foster a mechanism for their field personnel to fix corporate bottlenecks, which would have sounded an alarm in the '70s.

"But what about the cost of missing an entirely new market?"

Instead of looking at what Sears could get from the customer, they should have gotten closer to her and discovered that the customer's history and values were changing. They would also have learned that the story of the relationship between a customer and a catalog was timeless. They would have treated more than symptoms and focused on the cause of the customer's changing patterns. As a result, with their world leadership status at that time, they could have proactively led the customer and responded with agility and humility and had the edge in competing effectively with Walmart, The Home Depot, Best Buy, and Target. And, with just a touch of prescience they would have vanquished Amazon and Google.

"They would have treated more than symptoms and focused on the cause of the customer's changing patterns."

Frame of mind

Customer success delves into the mind of the customer. It goes beyond empathy. Empathy understands the customer from the customer's point of view. That's a good start—but not enough. Customer success analyzes what will catapult the customer to the next level.

Customer success is extraordinarily proactive. It anticipates what the customer will need—in many cases, prior to the customer's knowledge of their own need. Apple, Amazon, and Google are standout examples of pulling this off. In fact, the common thread between them and the reason for their extraordinary valuation is that they were conceived on the foundation of customer success, and they continue to grow because it is in the DNA of everything they do. Customer success also engages the emotions and strives for a positive experience for everyone involved. It is not limited to the well-worn sermons on customer service. Providing the customer with outstanding service of the wrong thing does not make him successful. The corporate ambition should be simple: anticipate the customer's real needs and provide genuine solutions that assist the customer beyond his expectations.

"Providing the customer with outstanding service of the wrong thing does not make him successful."

A customer service organization is tempted to let whatever is happening today dictate results. The customer success endeavor is attentive to the opportunities available and seizes the day. For an example, see Otto's Auto Repair Shop in Appendix C.

***

Customer success goes beyond customer service. It will:

1. Discover the customer's values and history.
2. Anticipate the customer's real needs.
3. Resolve the customer's symptoms and address the root cause.
4. Go beyond what is customary—do a backflip.
5. Lead the customer.
6. Respond quickly and with agility.
7. Exude a humble posture and remain diligent.

Chapter 3: Principle-Based Business

"We have always found that if our principles were right, the area over which they were applied did not matter." — Henry Ford

There is a generosity to the free market. When an entrepreneur or established business takes a risk and invests in a new product or service, he provides something that was previously not there. He adds value.

The principled business is focused on adding value. Of course, the business must make a profit. We drive to free cash flow and attempt to adopt the capital allocation concepts learned from the CEOs described in Harvard Business Review Press's *The Outsiders*, by William Thorndike Jr.

Still, one of the most pragmatic decisions a business leader can make is to build his business on a set of unchangeable principles. Dr. Henry Cloud's book *Integrity* is an excellent deep dive on the topic. This deliberate process has numerous benefits—chief among them is it provides a sound environment for our team to tell the truth before it is too late to fix something.

"One of the most pragmatic decisions a business leader can make is to build his business on a set of unchangeable principles."

When a first-time visitor flies into New York, on the long approach with a continuous view of Manhattan, you don't hear them say, "My, what impressive foundations this city has constructed." That's because all of us are impressed by what we see first.

Your customer is the same way. He doesn't first look at your philosophy statement. He notices the degree to which your receptionist is conscientious and respectful. That customer touchpoint is the equivalent of the skyscraper. Your principles are the foundation. The customer might not know your business principles, but he will certainly experience the fruits of their presence.

The four business principles on which my businesses are built are customer success philosophy, business methodology philosophy, values, and focus.

1. Customer success philosophy

"Get out and really listen to your customers." —Robert W. Galvin, 1988

The customer success philosophy is the bedrock principle. When our teams build upon this proactive approach, it permeates everything we do and everything else fits into place. It is how we render a hospitable environment to our only real corporate asset: the customer. This principle transcends the difficulties of everyday business. The customer success philosophy is critical to our way of thinking and our whole approach to every business decision. Chapter 1 elaborated on our customer success philosophy. It is not a formula; it is a mindset.

2. Business methodology philosophy

"For whoever aids the society of men by his industry . . . is not to be reckoned among the idle." —*John Calvin, 1548*

Our business methodology philosophy contributes to our success in two ways. First, it provides accountability to our senior leadership team. For example, we say that we believe in a wise debt load. Because of our business philosophy, we have always ensured that our debt loads are measured with a realistic return on the debt that is higher than the cost of the debt, including estimated market risk.

Second, a solid business philosophy keeps employees consistent and, more importantly, sets them free to solve problems. They have confidence to make intelligent business decisions. They do not have to apologize for any business conduct as it conforms to our business methodology philosophy.

Our business methodology philosophy is stated in terms of beliefs:

We believe in fundamental business ethics. We treat vendors, trusted advisors, customers, and employees the same way we want them to treat us.

We believe in the spirit of enterprise. We enjoy delivering exceptional business solutions and relish winning in the marketplace.

We believe in persistence. We push through the "hard." We believe there is a solution to the problem. We remind ourselves that the faint-hearted quit moments before the sale is closed or the innovation is discovered.

We believe in leadership. We seek intelligent counsel, but do not hesitate to make decisions. We distribute leadership broadly and deeply, providing authority and responsibility for the decision.

We believe in investing in people. We train, develop, and equip our staff with the tools to have the skill and passion for serving the customer with excellence. We reward them to embrace this attitude.

We believe in balanced tension. We believe in planning and analyzing the potential consequences of all business decisions, but we reject indecision due to lack of information. The left brain is important for analysis of data, but we also need the right brain to capture the intuitive component of business acumen.

We believe in wise debt loads. We believe debt should be used as a tool to increase the return on investment, but reject speculative leverage, since it carries unnecessary risks and unnecessarily burdens leadership with false choices.

We believe in the effective stewardship of time. Effectiveness does first things first. We resist the allure of easy lower priority tasks.

We believe in the effective stewardship of money. Efficiency evaluates expenditures under the microscope of return on investment. We invest in expansion, new projects, or acquisitions in terms of a probable return above the cost of debt or equity. We take thoughtful risks, but we think lean.

We believe in simplicity and common sense. We believe in focusing on the core services of our business, not being distracted by the vast array of lower margin possibilities. We endeavor to deploy our effort to service that we can deliver better than anyone else.

3. Driven by values

"Without a vision, the people perish." —Proverbs 29:18

Values are perhaps the most important component of the foundation for customer success. Values can be stated in a variety of ways. In my view they should highlight the Golden Rule: "Treat others as you want them to treat you."

The three values that we use to make customer success possible are integrity, innovation, and invitation. We structure them as declarative statements *to the customer*. For more detail on how these values connect to the definition of customer success, please see Appendix D.

Integrity

We do what we say we're going to do when we say we are going to do it, even when you are not watching, providing you with solutions that are whole and complete.

Innovation

With intellectual curiosity, we dig deeper and often uncover the best solutions after the project has commenced, delivering to you exceptional quality and unexpected value on budget.

Invitation

We create an inviting, collaborative, and drama-free work environment that motivates our employees to jump out of bed to come to work, is a magnet for top talent, and draws new clients to some of the best services they will ever experience.

When your values are clear, you have a foundation on which to build a great customer experience for your product or service. Capturing this in a vision statement answers the question "How do you want customers to feel?" This is discussed at length in my book *The Magic Wand*, but at the end of the day, we want an objective, measurable customer experience vision, developed from empowering questions, that guides our team to provide our customers with a great experience that garners their loyalty. Here is an example:

"GTT delivers seamless, specialized, talent solutions that meet client needs in an exceptional manner, and we enhance professional growth with integrity. We deliver these services with excellence resulting in referrals that drive our double-digit growth."

4. Focus on your purpose

"The secret of success is constancy of purpose." —Benjamin Disraeli, 1872

Our next principle is focus. This has to do with *concentrating single-mindedly on your corporate purpose.* It is easy to get distracted from your core competencies since you could probably be successful at many things. But to be exceptional at anything, you must focus.

However, the compulsion to diversify is seductive. At one time, Ford Motor Company owned and directly managed all aspects of their business. It even had its own sheep farm, from which it would take the wool to place in the car seat cushions. That was unwise. Now, they outsource almost everything except car design and marketing.

The seeds of this outsourcing concept were well articulated by Adam Smith in *The Wealth of Nations.* In the rudimentary state there is no "division of labor." One man's labor is rarely exchanged for another's. The individualist must be able to do everything in order to survive. When hungry, he goes outside and hunts. When his clothes wear out, he clothes himself with the skin of an elk or a bear.

When the division of labor is introduced, the wants and needs of the average person are supplied by the produce of another man's labor. If you prefer to go it alone, you might be able to survive in the wilderness, but not in the jungle of the marketplace. Adam Smith's concept, *the division of labor,* has resulted in productivity gains unimaginable in his day.

But, there is more to the concept. Adam Smith's contemporary David Ricardo introduced "comparative advantage" in 1817. The idea is as follows: if one state, like Iowa, is better at producing and selling corn than wheat, but it can produce and sell both wheat and corn, what should it do? According to Ricardo, it should sell corn and buy the wheat from its competitor in Kansas. You may be able to do both, but you will come out ahead if you focus on what you are comparatively much better at than your competitor. His concept of *comparative advantage* has been proven empirically. It just needs a free market. Hundreds of millions of people worldwide have risen out of poverty with blazing speed even though freedom economics principles have been implemented imperfectly.

The fastest growing, most profitable companies know their bent, and they ruthlessly set aside distractions. Here are two practical ways to abide by the principle of focus and the concept of comparative advantage.

"The fastest growing, most profitable companies know their bent, and they ruthlessly set aside distractions."

First, delegate smart. Keep the internal cost structure lean. And that often means outsourcing cost centers. Cost centers are the areas that must be managed, but regardless of how effectively they are managed, they are not going to generate more revenue for your business. In many companies this includes functions such as payroll, benefits administration, accounting, and human resource paperwork. In other companies it can include software development, manufacturing, assembly, distribution, and shipping.

The danger zones are in industries that you feel you can competently perform in-house. That is technically true, but how much money did Ford save managing sheep when they were supposed to be focused on designing and selling cars? Anything that requires management expertise, energy, and effort that does not support your purpose, you should consider delegating or outsourcing.

I am not suggesting that you blindly pay a vendor to manage one of your cost centers. When you delegate a function, you must stay involved. The vendor needs to be an ally. And you can structure the alliance with incentives that ensure you are well served. However, I am suggesting that when you have properly defined the areas that do not generate reasonable margin revenues, delegate them.

Second, give your team authority to stick with your comparative advantage. Often your customer will be attempting to share with you that they have an idea for you. And the idea is right in the middle of your purpose. But they don't come out and say, "Hey, I have an idea on how you can make more money on *me* and not lose me as a customer." Usually, it gets disclosed in a clumsy fashion, and very often it is a complaint against how one of your corporate bottlenecks have interfered with your purpose. If you give your team authority and responsibility to *Go Ahead* and fix the corporate bottleneck, you may be concurrently keeping a smaller, more agile competitor at bay.

"If you give your team authority and responsibility to Go Ahead and fix the corporate bottleneck, you may be concurrently keeping a smaller, more agile competitor at bay."

This may sound more like a business strategy than a business principle, yet it is based on the key principle of avoiding distractions that would render an inferior product or service to your customer. This is all about customer success, since the focused company generates more good margin revenue from its focus. A focused alliance forces necessary discipline on the company to go deeper with its core competencies, its comparative advantage, rather than skimming the surface of too many areas.

"A focused alliance forces necessary discipline on the company to go deeper with its core competencies, its comparative advantage, rather than skimming the surface of too many areas."

Fostering the entrepreneurial spirit

One mark of a business based on principles is an innovative mindset among your team. John Mill, a political economist in the mid-1800s, said, "All good things which exist are the fruits of originality." Well, maybe not everything, but when your team knows that you are committed to principles, they will emanate an entrepreneurial spirit. Your team will not have to be coaxed into delivering excellent service to their customers.

Here is a picture of what is going on in the mind of a customer success representative: "Last year, we were able to provide you with a useful service for your employee communications program. And though I am grateful that it was beneficial, wait until I share what we can offer now! I have been thinking about your situation and developed an even better solution. You might have to stretch just a bit to implement it properly, but it will yield a higher margin solution for you." Even the customer is being encouraged to think in new ways to improve his situation. This customer success representative has a passion for his customer's success.

Innovative thinking is contagious. We are not talking about introducing something new just because it is different. It must trump previous performance. Often, this is just a tweak of an already well-run process.

There is more to this than innovation. The concept of fostering the entrepreneurial spirit places greater responsibility on the customer success representative— but also provides her with greater rewards. If the business problem is the baby, then she is the mother, not just the babysitter.

"The concept of fostering the entrepreneurial spirit places greater responsibility on the customer success representative—but also provides her with greater rewards. If the business problem is the baby, then she is the mother, not just the babysitter."

There are times when an organization needs to be aroused from its slumber and undergo radical change. However, if the status quo is continually challenged, the shifts are caused by all the employees within the enterprise and they appear less radical. Change is not a *project* in the customer success environment. The entrepreneurial spirit becomes part of the daily routine. And the get-it-done culture is the best way to mitigate against disruption— where a smaller, more agile competitor introduces a new way of doing things.

By employing these concepts, your team will compete against itself and fill the customer's changing needs and desires before the smaller competitor's plan can be implemented. You'll always be changing, but you won't get "disrupted" out of business.

"By employing these concepts, your team will compete against itself and fill the customer's changing needs and desires before the smaller competitor's plan can be implemented. You'll always be changing, but you won't get 'disrupted' out of business."

***

A principle-based business is the best way to run a company for long-term success. It accounts for and incorporates the following:

1. A customer success philosophy
2. A business methodology philosophy
3. Values: integrity, innovation, invitation
4. Focus on your purpose

Chapter 4: Retaining the Right Customers

"Your most unhappy customers are your greatest source of learning." —Bill Gates

For customer success to flourish, the arc of the effort that your people expend should be focused on the customers that will reward your efforts. In a B2B environment, you have some control over who you will serve. In a B2C setting, the concepts in this chapter can be helpful to the design of your pricing and service delivery.

"For customer success to flourish, the arc of the effort that your people expend should be focused on the customers that will reward your efforts."

The right employees will help you keep the right customers, but there are customers that can severely damage your business. (Chapters 5 and 6 describe how to hire and train the right employees.) So, we want to focus on establishing an energetic environment where we get and keep customers that add value to the company.

Grading your customers

There are "A," "B," and "C" (and worse!) quality customers. An "A" customer pays you a proper amount for what you are offering them and genuinely appreciates your product or services. They buy your ice cream, pay your high-margin cost per scoop, and tell their friends how good it is. You have an excellent rapport with them, and they are gold. "B" customers are almost as good, but may be lacking in one or two of the above characteristics. "C" customers are a different matter.

You don't want every customer you can get. Some customers demand $10 of service for every $7 they are willing to pay. Some customers are just plain ornery. I have made the mistake of doing business with a rascal or two. While I've been in the process of performing a backflip for them, they find something else to bewail. They cannot possibly be satisfied. In fact, they are abusive. They are rude and incorrigible, and often they lie. In some cases, their unethical behavior will put your business in jeopardy. They need a spanking!

It is rare, but if necessary, our employees will cancel a customer. Normally, we just raise the price to the level where they leave on their own. The "C" (and worse) customers will have an adverse impact on your employees' morale. When your employees are overworked and underappreciated, they may eventually begin to treat even your "A" customers with disdain. In addition, the business leader will lose his focus.

"When your employees are overworked and underappreciated, they may eventually begin to treat even your 'A' customers with disdain."

Several years ago, one of our businesses took on a "C" customer that eroded to an "F-." This customer became one of the worst distractions in our company's history. And we were in the infancy stages of establishing one of our offices.

Why did we get snookered into this business relationship? We wanted to establish a presence in this new market so earnestly that it blinded us to the nearly impossible odds stacked against us. Unfortunately, we were willing to look past some of our own business advice to get there. We were set up to fail. If we had not disassociated with this customer, we would still be performing exceptional service for this one abusive customer at the expense of the rest of our business.

If you end up performing backflips for the "C" customer, two things will happen: you will get no applause, and your business will be directed by him, not you. A large list of "C" customers can absorb so much of your time that they will dictate how fast you grow and how profitable you become. In the B2B world, most "C" customers eventually go out of business. Where does this leave yours?

Financial weakness, of course, is the other indicator of a "C" customer. They may think your services are fabulous, but if they can't pay you, they should not be a customer. This can develop over time. They may start out as an "A" customer and eventually pay late or stop paying. Identify this early, and part ways as friends.

Our professional employer organization serviced a customer that was a pleasure in most ways for four years. Then the customer encountered financial difficulty. If I had graciously canceled our business relationship at this time, I would have escaped without a scratch. But I hung in there with him. When it was all said and done, he gave me some of his tow trucks. By the time I sold those, I lost money and a significant amount of time and energy. What would have happened if we had placed all that effort into finding more "A" customers or built up our "B" customers?

Software exists to help grade the customer in terms of profitability and value to your organization, but the point is to position the business so you primarily have "A" and "B" customers. We simply attempt to be watchful in both the sales cycle and the operations and service setting. We look for certain characteristics that have served us well to date. For example, "The last time contract negotiations went in this direction, it did not turn out well." If we detect a potential problem, we will look for a way to increase pricing or a contract issue to mitigate against the potential problem. For example, we will include in the contract the ability to make adjustments for unexpected surges in service.

If we bring on a customer and later wish we had not done so, we first attempt to fix the customer. We provide a formal appraisal of the value proposition to the customer mid-project. If he is paying us too little, we explain that as objectively as possible by providing a table of value items compared to his cost. If he is unwilling to allow us to make a reasonable profit, after we complete the current project with excellence, we graciously terminate the relationship. Usually, we just charge quite a bit more for the next phase. Sometimes that means a more formal discussion of why. And we level with him.

Keeping your customers

We endeavor to keep 100 percent of our "A" and "B" customers. When one of my companies lost any of these customers to a competitor, we quickly looked at our approaches and service offering. We sound the alarm and determine if we have any systemic problems in our business.

To position our business to increase the probability of successfully keeping our customers, our employees must live by five practices (based on our business principles):

1. *Sell with Integrity.* It is important to stick with your core competencies, your comparative advantage, and not to oversell by setting false expectations. The best way to lose customers or get financially skinned is to establish a standard above what you can deliver. If one of our salespeople conveys ten things that we can do, but we can really only do nine,

what happens? The other nine exceptional services are overshadowed in the mind of the customer by the one service failure.

There is another element to selling with integrity: positioning with purpose and truth. The purpose is to understand the actual objectives of the customer and deliver to that. If you can't deliver, you should pass. But proper positioning also means skillfully telling the truth. That usually means it costs more than the customer wants to pay. The objective is to persuade someone to buy your product or to use your service based on its actual performance and a reasonable profit margin. It does not require skill to give stuff away. More on this in chapter 8.

Surprisingly, most salespeople and business developers don't sell that well. They take orders. Selling with integrity adds value by uncovering the actual objectives of the customer. And it competently goes deep with a specific solution. As a result, you charge a fair margin for your products and services.

2. ***Serve with Innovation.*** Once you have obtained a customer, strive to eclipse their expectations. Do this based on a carefully thought-out plan of value-added services you can provide.

If you are in retail, think through the entire service delivery process and deliver—lack of execution of the customer's expectation is why one barbecue joint goes under just around the corner from one that thrives and has a line out the door. Rudy's, one of the highest revenue per foot restaurants in Texas, uses wax paper as plates and cheap chairs you can find at Goodwill! But the expectation of the customer is met flawlessly.

Our employees go all out to orient the customer to our business. We address concerns, and we provide easy access to customer success representatives. The first impression is critical, but we keep it up. Our goal is to make working with us a pleasure. We attempt to continually think through new processes, learn new skills, and use new tools to benefit the customer.

3. ***Coach with Integrity.*** A component of integrity is when the leader or owner is willing to be honest about his own shortcomings. When the leader has a proper self-estimate and can admit his own mistakes, this builds trust and inspires the team to action. Better than giving a list of rules, instill a desire to keep your "A" and "B" customers. Inculcate a belief that customer retention (as we define it) is worth the effort. The worst encounter for a customer is to be confronted with a customer service representative who does not really believe it matters—she doesn't care about retaining the customer.

"The worst encounter for a customer is to be confronted with a customer service representative who does not really believe it matters."

In sports, what makes the most difference in the outcome? Talent and coaching. If the talent is basically equal, coaching is what separates the winner from the loser. In particular, the degree to which the players trust the coach's plan determines the outcome.

The America's Cup is a sailing competition and the oldest trophy in international sport. The winner is the first one to reach nine wins in a "best of seventeen" head-to-head structure. In 2013, the race was seemingly a slam dunk for New Zealand. They were ahead eight races to one. With just one more win, New Zealand would take the Cup. Surprisingly, Team USA went on to win all eight of the remaining races to win 9-8—almost an oddsmaker's impossibility and still regarded as one of the greatest comebacks in all of sports history in any sport.

The first three legs of each race played to New Zealand's advantage, while the fourth leg was all Team USA, which gave them hope that they could turn things around. When Team USA lost race after race and were down eight to one, you'd think they would have given up. One more win for New Zealand and it was all over. However, Team USA did not panic even when, in each of those seventeen races (winning nine to eight), they were behind for 75 percent of the race. Why? Because of great coaching and great technology and a total belief in each other, Team USA was able to adjust to their skipper's directions and follow the plans that worked to their advantage.

In the marketplace, you must have a winning plan, too. The role of leadership is to inspire everyone to desire to and believe you can retain your key customers.

4. ***Recruit with Invitation.*** Hire employees who mirror your work ethic and ambition. (More on this in chapter 5.) Enable your employees to think like an owner. As discussed in *The Magic Wand*, design your culture and compensation structure around providing them with the responsibility and authority to perform a backflip for the customer. Even the best coach in any sport must have good talent to succeed. Make sure your employees can embrace your values. Most have not thought about the values they want in a work environment, but they are willing to adopt yours. Look for skilled people who readily adopt integrity,

63

innovation, and invitation (or your own rendition of it) as part of their work lives.

5. ***Retain with Invitation.*** We motivate our internal staff financially and emotionally, because we believe there is a direct connection between employee retention and customer retention. We do everything we can to keep our people.

Customer retention is not a project. It is a company-wide environment that produces a symbiotic effect: employee retention feeds customer value and customer value nourishes employee retention. The invitation mantra encompasses a cultural plan to make the work environment as enjoyable and challenging as possible.

Why is employee retention linked to customer retention? As customers, we are all basically the same. When provided with a choice, we buy from the person we like the best. The same is true with repeat purchases and ongoing service. We like to interact with the person who knows our story and adapts his services to our particular needs. We would rather not explain our needs again and have to train another person on how to serve us. When a good employee leaves an organization, two things happen. The customer wonders if there is a management problem "over there," and he loses the person he prefers to deal with.

"We like to interact with the person who knows our story and adapts his services to our particular

needs. We would rather not explain our needs again and have to train another person on how to serve us."

Laying the groundwork

OK. You're sold on customer success. You want your customers to lavish you with praise. You love tweaking your service delivery to improve flow and delight your customers so they buy more high-margin ice cream from you.

You are committed to empowering your people with authority. So how do you get your employees to follow suit? Wouldn't it be nice if you could establish a mechanism that not only created a customer success environment, but also perpetuated itself without artificial props? This is the exciting promise that fostering a customer success mindset can bring to your organization.

This next section presents some specific training suggestions for helping employees implement a new approach.

- *Begin with the right people or it will fail.* You can be the best trainer and have the best material, but the employee must possess basic qualities. (Chapters 5 and 6)
- *It must be simple and clear to work.* Boundaries need to be clear, but the freedom to act within the

65

boundaries should be strong. More important, the direct supervisors of the customer success agents must be fully onboard and aligned with you. (Chapter 9)

- *It must have meaning*. If we simply dish out new duties, we do not change the employee's mindset. Explaining the *why* of the duty is as important as explaining the how-to. (Chapter 9)

- *It must be modeled.* The boss must exemplify the desired behavior. The customer success mindset is caught when an employee observes his supervisor providing exceptional service delivery. (Chapter 7)

"If we simply dish out new duties, we do not change the employee's mindset."

***

To sustain the customer success mindset, you also need to:

---

1. "Grade" your customers.
2. Focus on "A" and "B" customers.
3. Sell with integrity.
4. Serve with innovation.
5. Coach with integrity.
6. Recruit with invitation.
7. Retain with invitation.

Part Two: A Customer Success Mindset

Chapter 5: Hiring Go Ahead! People

"In looking for people to hire, you look for three qualities: integrity, intelligence, and energy. And if you don't have the first, the other two will kill you." —Warren Buffett

Our software engineering firm (MSL) was part of the first billion-dollar software contract with the Air Force, helping to upgrade NORAD's radar and satellite systems. We won our part of that contract because of our people.

Initially, we founded that business with basically nothing, except for a talented co-founder, Randy, my capital, and these three fantastic tech guys: Al, Mike, and Craig. They may have been among the best in the world at their trade. Somehow, we were able to convince them we would build a great culture. (My first book, *Customer Success*, was produced six months after hiring these guys, but the philosophy had already been in practice in my PEO business.)

They were also good people—men of solid character. It was natural for them to develop, think, and invent to the benefit of the customer. But, to do that in advance of winning the contract was a special adaptation of proactively thinking about what would be best for the customer. When we won the contract three years later, they helped us find dozens of other like-minded and capable professionals.

Earlier, I mentioned that the greatest corporate assets are customers. This can be substantiated in the enormous valuations for many high-tech companies like Twitter and Facebook years before they were profitable. The market rewards companies that have customers with demonstrated loyalty.

The customer is the greatest asset, but that doesn't mean you put your customers first. We focus on our team. Exceptional employees make wonderful things happen. We look for *Go Ahead* people. These individuals are willing to own the customer. They might not understand all the values up front, but they have the character to enjoy the challenge of proactive service—they are enthusiastic promoters of the solution for the customer.

Without Al, Mike, and Craig, we could not have convinced one of the largest customers in the world to buy services from us. Twelve years later we sold that business to the NASA Hubble Telescope contractor and delivered to our investor a triple digit compound return on investment. We can't overstate how important it is to get the right people.

"We can't overstate how important it is to get the right people."

And this is where customer success becomes contagious—where the weight of the culture is bent toward an uplifting, energetic, proactive environment that benefits the customer. Hiring the right people generates internal advocates who apply positive peer pressure.

So, take your time up front. The hiring process is outside the scope of this book, but here are eight practices to consider.

1. *Allocate strategic energy to detail the behavioral traits of success of the job.* In addition to the basic duties, we endeavor to think through the natural traits that would be most likely to help a candidate succeed. For example, do they need to be deductive or inductive thinkers? Do they need to be more extroverted or introverted to be successful in this job? Do they need to be more linear or creative?

2. *Use the RASCI chart in the interview.* The RASCI table normally isn't used in the recruiting process. It is designed to ensure each assignment has an owner and to make sure things are not slipping through the cracks. There are hundreds of examples of RASCI tables easily accessible. But consider using it to help identify the next recruit and flush out some of the details of working relationships during the interview process. Map out what he will be responsible (R) for, what he will need to have

power to approve (A), what he will need to support (S), what would benefit the business for him to help in a consultative (C) role, and what he will need to inform (I) us of.

If you are going to use the RASCI table as a tool once the candidate is on board, why not use it during the interview process to make sure he is a good fit for what you believe he will actually do once you hire him? This proactive concept can add value. And, it is very customer success friendly. Going through the matrix during the interview process will transition the interview into more of a collaborative problem-solving discussion. It helps you talk about the job in light of the customer and his potential coworkers. It gets more real.

It can also help seal the deal. He may be concerned about the risk of leaving his current job, but he knows his skills are a great fit for the job. And he likes your customer success culture. But, taking him through this process allows him to more realistically envision what the job will entail.

3. *In certain situations, use a stress interview.* Simulate an environment of an exaggerated bad day at the job. For example, you may ask the candidate to complete a memo in twenty minutes while being interrupted by an irate customer. At the same time, inform her of an important sales meeting in fifteen minutes. Watch how the candidate prioritizes under

pressure. This provides a reasonably predictable picture of what the person is really like.

4. ***Provide the candidate with a working interview.*** This is an opportunity to come in for a day before the formal offer is finalized. It allows the candidate to look over your company more thoroughly before providing notice to his current employer. This allows him to assess your culture before making the jump. And it gives you a final chance to reconsider whether he is a good fit for you.

5. ***Advertise your culture.*** Ultimately, the best way to recruit is to remain true to your values. That is how we got Al, Mike, and Craig. We described the culture we wanted MSL to possess. When you advertise for a job, promote your culture: "We're not just offering you a job; we're offering you an opportunity to participate in a creative and innovative work environment" or "We provide a drama-free environment for technology whizzes to express their capabilities." Plus, you want folks who don't fit with your culture to self-select out of applying.

6. ***Verify integrity with a background check.*** This protects your company against negligent hiring, but it also verifies that he has integrity. Does the candidate really have a college degree? Is he really a Buckeye? Is he a convicted felon? I'm more interested in his honesty than I am in whether he worked at the company listed on his résumé.

7. ***Invest in an excellent onboarding process.*** This positions your new employee with a strong introduction to the company's values and orients him to relevant logistics. It sets him up for success. See Appendix F for some of our new hire orientation ideas.

8. ***Demonstrate how your company depends on customers.*** As part of onboarding or soon thereafter, teach her how you earn a profit. Explain what products and services are the most profitable. Explain the risks and opportunities you encounter. Define the value of the customer to your bottom line. Discuss how costly it is in marketing and service dollars to obtain and maintain a customer. Provide a profile of the company's customers. Describe how many customers you have, who they are, what they are like, where they are located, what makes them buy from you.

"Define the value of the customer to your bottom line."

Being able to hire the best people with both a high probability of success at the job and who possess integrity makes your job of implementing a customer success culture a whole lot easier. Senior leadership is now able to primarily focus its management time on encouraging and supporting them.

One final note. Tweak the behaviors of likely success for certain positions; you will eventually crack the code. We had previously been frustrated with our inability to predict success with the direct sales position. We finally figured out seven behaviors that more consistently predict success for that position. See Appendix E.

***

Here are some thoughts on hiring the right people and positioning them for success:

1. Detail the behavioral traits of success of the job.
2. Use the RASCI chart in the interview.
3. Conduct a stress interview.
4. Provide the opportunity for a working interview.
5. Advertise your culture.
6. Verify integrity with the background check.
7. Invest in an excellent onboarding process.
8. Demonstrate how your company depends on customers.

Chapter 6: Customer Success Culture

"The genius of American culture and its integrity comes from fidelity to the light. Plain as day, we say. Happy as the day is long. Early to bed, early to rise. American virtues are daylight virtues." —Richard Rodriguez

A customer success culture is productive, uplifting, and respectful. We spend over half of our waking hours at work. And it should be fun—a place we look forward to going to. It certainly should not add unnecessary relational stress. But the reality is most businesses are unnecessarily political. In order to unleash a customer success culture, make a deliberate plan to minimize conflict in your organization. Here's ours:

1. Employee relations are respectful, accountable, and uplifting.
2. Communication is clear and appropriate.
3. Everyone appreciates each other (warts and all).
4. Politics are not tolerated.

1. Employee relations are respectful, accountable, and uplifting.

To enjoy working hard, we need an environment where we treat one another right. We encourage creating and maintaining an environment that is based on the following employee relation guidelines:

- **Expect the best of your coworkers.** Commit to cooperation.
- **Convey appreciation for your colleagues' attributes.** Affirm each other often.
- **Be approachable.** Keep a pleasant expression on your face. It is hard to approach someone who looks grouchy.
- **Wholeheartedly rejoice when a colleague does well.** When you express envy, you violate a principle. When someone else has good fortune, go out of your way to congratulate him.
- **Refuse to be moody.** Temperamental people are inconsistent and unreliable. We all have ups and downs in our personal lives. Don't bring your problems to work.
- **Be humble.** The reality is none of us has all the answers. False modesty is not the solution. It is OK to have a reasonable self-assessment. Just don't be arrogant.

- **Don't gossip.** Critical talk about someone behind her back is destructive. Constructively face the person with whom you have a grievance.
- **Manage stress.** Don't let it manage you. The world is not going to end if you make a mistake. Take a deep breath, and face the problem.
- **Acknowledge mistakes.** Correct the error without making excuses.

2. Communication is clear and appropriate.

It is almost impossible to overcommunicate. Communication is critical, but it is pretty simple. We attempt to train our employees that conscientious communication respects and honors the individual on the receiving end and improves relationships with our internal and external stakeholders. A total of five components contribute to communication: sender, receiver, mode, message, and impact.

"We attempt to train our employees that conscientious communication respects and honors the individual on the receiving end and improves relationships with our internal and external stakeholders."

As the *sender*, what exactly is it you are attempting to convey? Do you want to gain sympathy, enlist trust, inspire commitment, or share gratitude?

The *receiver* is everything—the audience. Who is that person? What is he like? How well do you know him? How busy is he? Communicating to a receptionist requires the same level of respect but can be different than communicating to a CEO. The CEO is likely looking for the executive summary. The receptionist is often willing to hear more of the details.

Often, we don't think much about the appropriate *mode* for sending our message. We usually assume an email or text is fine. But that is not always true. For example, don't just email your corporate values to a new employee; discuss them in person.

Jac Fitz-enz of the Human Capital Source surveyed a major West Coast bank to discover how their employees wished to learn a variety of pertinent information. In almost every situation, the overwhelming preference was from the direct supervisor.

Encourage employees to ask themselves, "What is the right mode in which to send the message?"

What about the *message* that you are sending? Well-worded content is important, but I am also referring to the reasons for sending the message. Is this to gain support for a critical strategic initiative? To inform people about a new company procedure? To bring correction to an employee? To show that you have taken into account input from a subordinate? To prove to someone that you are not the ogre that they think you are? Sometimes the subtle reasons and hidden agendas of why you are sending a message can speak louder than the actual content. The subject line should be accurate and descriptive.

"*Sometimes the subtle reasons and hidden agendas of why you are sending a message can speak louder than the actual content.*"

The communication should have the *impact* that you intend. Did the communication actually motivate the receivers to measurable performance improvements? Are the employees more inspired? Did you really defuse the conflict that was brewing? Is the quality of service at a higher level? Is there now a more dedicated workforce?

Leadership should be as transparent as is wise. I am not suggesting that you should share your merger plans. However, broadly share your vision, values, new customers, new services, new marketing plans, and operational enhancements. Effective and open communication helps employees buy in to the vision, and it helps them weather the storms.

Genuine communication engages the mind, but also the heart. If we communicate our belief that the equipped employee has permission to *Go Ahead* and get the job done it creates a platform to build reciprocal trust. If you have their trust, you can win their loyalty. Like Anthony Hope said in 1897, "Unless one is a genius, it is best to aim at being intelligible."

"Unless one is a genius, it is best to aim at being intelligible."

3. Everyone appreciates each other (warts and all).

To build a cohesive team, the employees need to have a general understanding of themselves and those they work with. There are numerous tools available to assess, define, and discuss the way people learn, what values are important to them, and why they do what they do. This exercise renders the ancillary benefit of training people to "read" customers. They become more skilled at handling the variety of personalities.

The DiSC test is one of many simple and easy-to-use personality tools. It uses an eight-minute test that produces a variety of reports. Essentially, the personality characteristics break down into four basic categories, abbreviated as DISC:

- **Dominance**—This person places an emphasis on shaping the environment by overcoming opposition to accomplish results. This person will cause action, challenge the status quo, and solve problems. He might be weak in researching the facts, calculating the risks, and understanding the needs of others.
- **Influence**—This person is interested in influencing or persuading others. She will be a natural at verbalizing, contacting people, and generating enthusiasm. She

might be a bit weak in speaking directly, focusing on the task at hand, and following through.

- **Steady**—This person places a high emphasis on cooperating with others to carry out tasks. He will be gifted at developing specialized skills, creating a stable, harmonious work environment, and performing in a constant, predictable fashion. He will not be naturally good at reacting quickly to unexpected change, applying pressure on others, or conveying flexibility in work procedures.

- **Conscientious**—This person is interested in working well within existing circumstances to ensure quality and accuracy. She is good at thinking analytically, focusing on details, and being diplomatic with people. She needs encouragement to delegate important tasks, to be flexible with policies, and to encourage teamwork.

We discuss the results in a group of direct reports or associates that interact on a regular basis. We inject humor when we point out that all personality styles have some weaknesses—we all have warts. This opens the door for us to protect and defend each other with our complementary strengths. We discuss how we could potentially perceive the same task differently. It turns out to be great fun for everyone and enables our leaders to equip our employees to work together more effectively.

"This opens the door for us to protect and defend each other with our complementary strengths."

People are positioned in advance to not get bent out of shape over little things. When conveyed in an uplifting manner, they understand how to work with each other and how to leverage one another's strengths to deliver the best solution for the customer.

4. Politics are not tolerated.

When I say *politics*, I am not talking about prudent diplomacy. I am addressing the interactions among people that cause self-doubt and absorb emotional energy, where colleagues take sides, play favorites, and criticize behind each other's backs. It is destructive, so we endeavor to destroy politics. Company politics will erode a customer success environment faster than any other single company weakness.

"Company politics will erode a customer success environment faster than any other single weakness."

In all business settings, people have "bad hair" days. Let's take two peers who are under stress. We will call them Jim and Ann. Jim is in the midst of resolving a difficult customer problem. Ann needs Jim's attention now, prior to making an important decision. Their high-stress moments collide. They have the beginnings of a conflict.

Typically, no work rule requires fellow employees to resolve a conflict. But that creates an open door for things to play out unproductively with Jim and Ann.

The friction intensifies, and their business relationship erodes. Two weeks ago, these people shared a mutual respect. Now, they are adversaries looking for a way to expose each other's weaknesses. Jim builds up his "kingdom," while Ann establishes her "queendom." He rallies to form against hers, and she establishes a network that opposes him. He defames her, and she slanders him. Previously overlooked quirks are highlighted.

If they are both candidates for the same promotion, the best person won't win. The least manipulative and least politically adept of the two will lose. Let's say the loser is Jim. If he is influential, he will persuade his comrades of the corporation's unfair and evil ways. Ann moves up but is always looking over her shoulder.

What happens to the tone of these two employees or their subordinates when a customer calls? The attitudes harbored by these employees will leak to the customer. Ever wonder why a well-organized customer service program is next to impossible to maintain? If you don't destroy politics, politics will destroy the fabric of your organization.

"If you don't destroy politics, politics will destroy the fabric of your organization."

In our companies, we nipped this type of behavior in the bud. It is a verbally stated job requirement to resolve an offense as soon as practical. In some general meeting, it is regularly conveyed by a senior leader. Unless there is an emergency, employees must handle conflict before the close of the business day.

Before the conflict arises, we instruct them as follows: The two people in conflict must get into a private office and close the door. We convey that we expect them to be professional enough to initiate this on their own, without the knowledge of anyone else. There is a high possibility the entire matter is based in faulty communication. One party kicks things off with four words: "I may be wrong." She then continues, "I was just trying to get a piece of information that only you possess. In my view you were unnecessarily gruff with me. Did I perceive this incorrectly?"

The other person must respond with humility as well. He says, "I may be wrong. I didn't mean to convey any malice. I am so focused on this project that I might have been abrupt, but I sure didn't mean anything by it." Usually, it stops right there. In thirty seconds we have intercepted the establishment of two enemy empires within our midst.

I understand you might be skeptical, but since 1996, I have had very few actual closed-door sessions in any of the companies I have run. Just the threat of a requirement to destroy politics eliminates most problems at the source.

But what if the discussion above did not result in an amiable resolution? What next? The immediate supervisor functions as the referee. He listens to both sides privately and then brings them together and resolves the problem. He is skilled in due process and getting to the heart of the matter. He knows how to ask good questions and bring resolution, not simply determine a winner. The victor doesn't get the kids while the loser gets the boat. These rare situations are used to strengthen our corporate culture. But he doesn't make it easy on either one. By the way, we have had only a dozen or so of these in over two decades of employing the concept.

What if there is still no resolution? If one of the employees continues to feel that her complaint was not properly managed, she can elevate the arbitration all the way up to the CEO. This has only happened a handful of times.

Employees could abuse a grievance procedure and use the process to drain their supervisors. That has never happened in my businesses. We don't permit the conniving manipulator to gain control of the business. That is a leadership thing—we train ours to ensure this process destroys politics rather than establishes them. If the process is elevated, the leader's first question is: "What was the result of stage one? How did you start your first sentence?"

We are trying to make it hard to hold on to petty issues. And we make it fatal (from a career-with-us standpoint) to become a retaliating employee. We are very clear about it up front.

"We are trying to make it hard to hold on to petty issues. And we make it fatal (from a career-with-us standpoint) to become a retaliating employee."

The results have been great. People prefer to do their job without needing to look over their shoulder. You don't need to allow gossip, backstabbing, slander, or triangulation methods to negatively impact your work environment. Establish a procedure that enables relationship concerns to be quickly resolved based on your business principles. Implement employee relations that support a customer success culture and destroy (or prevent) politics. This enables your employees to focus on productive value-added efforts. And when your employees are successful, so are your customers.

***

The keys to a customer success culture are:

1. Employee relations are respectful, accountable, and uplifting.
2. Communication is clear and appropriate.
3. Everyone appreciates each other (warts and all).
4. Politics are not tolerated.

Chapter 7: Cohesion Starts at the Top

"You do not lead by hitting people over the head—that's assault, not leadership." —Dwight Eisenhower

The overused term "servant leader" is still the best leadership style. These leaders assert themselves with a genuine outcome goal of encouraging, strengthening, and equipping the team for out-of-the-ordinary accomplishments. The team that wins is not necessarily the one with the most superstar athletes; it's the one where the athletes give it their all and move in sync. To enjoy the rewards of a customer success environment, the management team and all the key business leaders must be moving toward the same purpose. When business leaders work together, the rest of the organization can focus on efforts that are in the customer's best interest. A few key ingredients establish the leadership culture required to achieve a lasting customer success environment.

"These leaders assert themselves with a genuine outcome goal of encouraging, strengthening, and equipping the team for out-of-the-ordinary accomplishments."

Have fun.

I really want to provide a great work environment for our employees. We don't play pinball during work hours, but we do encourage laughter. There is a difference between fun and play. We do not play at work. But, for crying out loud, the majority of our waking life will be spent at work! So, rather than make work drudgery, we find ways to shape the environment, enabling the grind of the workday to be enjoyable.

"We don't play pinball during work hours, but we do encourage laughter."

Our leaders encourage our associates to contribute to a pleasant working environment. We do not have a specific incentive system tied to a "fun-o-meter," but since the businesses I have run primarily offer services that the customer takes very seriously, it is important that we find ways to brighten up the workday for each other. Anyone who has the desire may devise appreciation lunches, birthday celebrations, etc. We encourage this because we want the employees to enjoy one another, but I am not suggesting frivolity. Another word for happiness is satisfaction. To be satisfied with a job well done is an environment where others celebrate your success—that's fun!

Schedule a bit of pleasure mixed with your business. This starts at the top. In one of our businesses, my senior vice presidents and I would get together for a weekend retreat (Friday and Saturday) about three times a year. First, we work. We get the majority of our agenda finished on Friday. Then, we play. We ski, snowmobile, golf, or play basketball. We meet in a nice place, have good food, and discuss business issues or whatever else at each meal. While our goal is not to have fun—ski, golf, etc.—we do have fun. With the proper amount of discipline, we accomplish the agenda. Since we are relating in a different context, we can really enjoy one another as well as produce.

When the leaders enjoy each other, they can accomplish almost anything. The leaders will convey the essence of the enjoyment factor in the way they relate to their subordinates. They do not have to organize a host of fun extracurricular activities to pull this off. The leader simply models an excellent work ethic with the right demeanor. He is still serious about excellence; he just doesn't take himself too seriously.

Having fun is a responsibility to take seriously. In fact, it is good for you: "A joyful heart is good medicine," says Proverbs 17:22. It is like the basketball star who goes "unconscious" and doesn't miss a shot. Listen to athletes respond to an interview after an all-time high-scoring game. They make all of their shots not because they are super-serious about their technique but because they are having fun.

Cover for each other's weaknesses.

Normally, one manager thinks he will rise to the top faster if he can exploit the weakness of the other manager. He thinks, *Helping him certainly won't help me.*

Consider going against the grain of our culture, and encourage your managers to be looking out for each other's weaknesses. You probably doubt that this is possible. Our senior leaders have done it. This concept does not reduce healthy competition in any way. It actually strengthens your leaders and is very customer success friendly.

The CEO can make it clear that an aspiring leader will have more opportunity to enjoy growth if he looks out for the other guy. As a result, it is in his self-interest to watch his peer's backside.

To illustrate this point, envision four martial arts gurus defending themselves against twenty big, burly, but untrained bad guys. The four martial arts experts position themselves back to back, communicate extremely well, and rely on one another's directives about when to duck and when to hit. These trained fighting men will obtain almost certain victory if they function as a cohesive unit.

The big, burly, untrained bad guys represent the obstacles we must hurdle to render the right kind of service to our customers. The last thing our team needs is for one of our "martial arts experts" to bolt on us in our time of need.

Leaders have varying strengths. One key leader is probably the most disciplined, exemplifying orderliness and follow-through. Another key leader is the most direct, able to cut through issues with clarity and boldness. As these leaders sponsor one another, their corresponding strengths are an inspiration to everyone else. They can leverage each other's strengths to collaborate and solve customer problems.

"As these leaders sponsor one another, their corresponding strengths are an inspiration to everyone else."

This builds a level of trust that enhances your business's service capability. When some outsider points out a weakness about one of your key managers, you can quickly cover for him. This does not mean blithely *covering up* for him, but simply finding constructive ways to compensate for his weakness.

The leadership team must convey that the ticket to advancement is to work hard and focus on making our customers successful—not defeating someone else on the team. This is particularly true when it involves effectively covering for the weaknesses of your colleague. The CEO must communicate that one's talent and ability—without political maneuvering—will carve out a position that elevates an employee to his full potential.

"The CEO must communicate that one's talent and ability—without political maneuvering—will carve out a position that elevates an employee to his full potential."

Be loyal and trustworthy.

Loyalty and trust are in short supply. An excellent picture of loyalty and trust is found in the college basketball tradition of North Carolina. Bill Guthridge was an assistant coach for the team for thirty years. The famous head coach Dean Smith made sure he retired just before the 1997–1998 season got underway. This way he could ensure the administration would have no choice but to allow Bill to have a shot at the head coaching job.

In Bill's first year, he was named "Coach of the Year" and his team was ranked number one in the country going into the final NCAA tournament. We may have never known what Bill could do had Dean not paved the way for him. True to form, throughout his spectacular first year of coaching, Bill gave credit to Dean.

Almost everyone works below his or her potential. They may work very hard, long hours, but rarely do people max out on their capabilities. They hold back. The business leader's main objective should be to develop his people to a level that they otherwise would not have attained. When the employees realize that this is the leader's intention, they engage in useful collaboration with their peers.

Delegate authority and responsibility (risk).

We honor the relationship between authority and risk. This is closely connected to the concept of distributing authority as close to the customer as possible. That is superior to the centralized headquarters approach. Headquarters should be lean. At the end of the day, when you delegate an assignment or project or P&L responsibility, you must give them the authority to carry it out.

Adam (of Adam and Eve fame in the Bible) was given responsibility and authority for naming the animals. Here's proof: "And whatever the man called a living creature, that was its name" (Genesis 2:19). God didn't come back and say, "Wait a minute, Adam, you can't call that thing a zebra!" When God gave Adam the responsibility to name the animals, God gave him the authority to match the responsibility.

I wonder if Adam would have flunked the reference check because he had no related experience. God was willing to take a risk. Ronald Reagan said it well: "Surround yourself with the best people you can find, delegate authority, and don't interfere as long as the policy you've decided upon is being carried out."

"Surround yourself with the best people you can find, delegate authority, and don't interfere as long as the policy you've decided upon is being carried out."

Whether a business leader heads a department, a small consulting firm, or a multibillion-dollar corporation, releasing control is essential. To be successful in the long term, the business leader must delegate authority along with responsibility.

One of the worst dilemmas for any employee is to be saddled with responsibility and not possess sufficient authority to implement the solution. On the other hand, it is quite rewarding to be granted the power needed to manage a project. Granting authority unleashes innovation.

In one of my businesses, a woman joined the company as a part-time administrative assistant. She filed papers and ran errands. She was loyal, hard-working, faithful, and conscientious. While still a part-time employee, her direct supervisor asked her to locate and purchase an expensive piece of equipment. When she brought the top three options to him, he did not look at her comparison spreadsheet. He just asked her a few questions about her assumptions and methodology. Satisfied, he instructed her to make the best decision for the business and go ahead and order it. She couldn't believe it. She thought that she was just supposed to find the best solution. She later told him, "I want to thank you for trusting me with that decision. It is almost overwhelming that you gave me that much authority."

An environment that allows employees to *Go Ahead* and get it done makes owners out of your employees. They genuinely care deeply about the outcomes. And their increased fulfillment enhances employee retention.

"An environment that allows employees to Go Ahead and get it done makes owners out of your employees. They genuinely care deeply about the outcomes. And their increased fulfillment enhances employee retention."

By the way, she made a great purchasing decision—but she could have made a poor one. The business leader must embrace that risk.

Here is some support for that concept. All development, all originality, and all innovation begin with the destruction of something. If you want to build a house, you destroy certain areas of the natural environment. If you want to make one product, you consume others. If you want to render a service, you displace time or effort.

The Austrian economist Joseph Schumpeter eloquently demonstrated this reality. He called it creative destruction. At every level the risk of loss is necessary for innovation. In fact, with innovation old ideas and technologies become obsolete. Something has to be put at risk to gain the benefit of creativity.

"Something has to be put at risk to gain the benefit of creativity."

101

So my objective with this principle is to demonstrate that when business leaders are willing to take risks—as in delegating authority to their employees—innovation flourishes. Often the only direction I give to employees is, "What is the best business decision? *Go Ahead* and make it happen!"

"What is the best business decision? Go Ahead and make it happen!"

One of the most important things a leader can do is look in the eye of his subordinate and say, "I trust you. I will support you as long as your actions are in compliance with our philosophy." If you want your people to provide innovative solutions, they must be set free. This does not mean you are lenient on issues of prudence. To the contrary, releasing people puts them on the hook. They are more accountable because they can never use the excuse that they did not have sufficient authority to take advantage of an opportunity.

"If you want your people to provide innovative solutions, they must be set free."

We do recommend that their decisions be supported by using a sound process. For example, if the employee uses our company's problem-solving schematic, he might make a different decision than I would, but it is likely to be a good one. Embracing risk does not imply less due diligence. It does, however, avoid passing the buck.

At one of the large companies I used to work for, I was struck by how little power any one person really possessed. Someone would conceive a great idea, properly document it, and then refer it to another person up the food chain. Though the idea was compelling and within the next person's budget, he would make sure someone over him supported it. Amazingly, his superior made sure that enough other fingerprints were on the project that if it ever went awry, the blame would not fall on him. This is how talented people in large companies sometimes allocate more energy to covering their behinds than to generating bold new products and services. No one just says, *"Go Ahead!"*

"Talented people in large companies sometimes allocate more energy to covering their behinds than to generating bold new products and services."

We all are created with the capacity for some level of autonomy. That is why this principle has the associated benefit of increasing employee retention. Few things are more rewarding in a work setting than being set free to think outside the nine dots and move ahead with courage to try new ideas. Encourage them to *Go Ahead!* As your employees are free to devise innovative solutions, your customers will be thrilled beyond their expectations.

***

Implement these key ingredients to unleash a contagious customer success culture:

1. Have fun.
2. Cover each other's weaknesses.
3. Be loyal and trustworthy.
4. Delegate authority and responsibility (risk).

Part Three: The
Customer Success Way

Chapter 8: Getting Customers the Right Way

"Persuasion, kind unassuming persuasion, should be adopted to influence the conduct of men." —Abraham Lincoln

We believe that the way we go about increasing revenue matters. Marketing and sales should be laced with integrity—and a strong, value-added, persuasive reason to buy. It incorporates more than features and benefits. It answers the "why" of the purchase. That is the selling proposition.

Understanding your selling proposition can improve the odds of delivering customer success. And when you execute your services or deliver your product at or above the selling proposition, you make money. You meet or exceed expectations, and you have happy customers.

The operations team ensures that the customer is successful after the sale, but the sales professionals tee it up. For example, in a complex B2B sale, the team involved in post-close negotiations can do wonders for the company in setting expectations that the business can easily deliver.

Recall Rudy's, the exceptionally successful barbecue restaurant based in Texas. The customer's expectation is for fantastic brisket, not a five-star seating arrangement. And that expectation is met with very customer success minded cashiers. And you can come as you are—suit and tie from the office or grubbies from working in the yard. A restaurant with no plates, card tables, and a concrete floor has a line out the door, because they know their selling proposition. And they deliver at or above that expectation consistently.

> *"A restaurant with no plates, card tables, and a concrete floor has a line out the door, because they know their selling proposition. And they deliver at or above that expectation consistently."*

In a longer sales cycle such as a multi-year consulting project or medical equipment, the direct sales person sets the expectation for a successful implementation and a satisfied customer. It comes down to two things: selling with integrity and negotiating with value.

Sell with integrity

The sales team can help position the company for success before you have taken a nickel from the customer, and they will generate ideas that no one in operations would ever see.

I encourage operations people to go out on sales calls when possible, but usually the customer's first interaction with the company is with the business developer. The tone of selling with integrity is to find legitimate ways the service or product will help the customer succeed.

To accomplish this, train the sales staff to focus on identifying ways to interact with the prospects from a consultant's perspective and to sell with integrity. This means they are nonmanipulative but appropriately savvy; they get to the source objectives of the customer and effectively match those objectives to solutions the company can deliver with excellence.

They don't oversell, but they do persuade. In a complex setting, analyze the risks with the prospective customer early in the sales process. By conveying some of the risks of employing your service, you will unseat objections and establish credibility. Then assist them with evaluating those risks. Review with your prospective new customer each corresponding opportunity or value of using your service. When the analysis is complete, the prospective customer often decides that the opportunities outweigh the risks. And the sale sticks.

We combine our values with some elements of two approaches, one from Sandler Sales and one from IBM (see Appendix B for more detail on these sales methods). Sandler takes a nonmanipulative approach to getting in the door and not wasting time. They exercise discipline in the prequalification stage and throughout the process. They develop a large pipeline, but if the service or product is not of value to the potential customer, why drive all over town? They use a permission-laden approach that disarms the prospect. It also builds trust, grants the prospective customer legitimate power, and keeps the salesperson focused on real opportunities.

If the prospective customer wants to hear more, the approach requires lots of questions to find both the rational and the emotional triggers behind why the customer may want to buy. The salesperson probes for their real motivations, asking open-ended questions and listening. The salesperson continually gleans feedback from the potential customer to ensure he is not wasting his time. This approach reveals hidden authorities and false budgets and reduces the sales cycle time as well as improves the post-close success rate.

The IBM approach uses four simple concepts: rapport, customer objectives, customer solution, and close. The concept of establishing rapport is lost on some—but IBM's traditional method teaches eye contact and genuine interest in the person. No one wants to buy from someone they don't like. The salesperson needs the emotional maturity to genuinely care about the customer personally. From there, he can build trust and uncover what the real issues are with the prospective customer. Once the salesperson learns the customer's objectives, generated from thought provoking questions, he uses a problem-solving schematic (we have our simple version in chapter 9) to educate the customer on how the company's approach will solve their problems. Then he directly asks for the business.

We have combined Sandler and IBM's approach to build a seven- step process. The seven steps are:

1. Build and qualify the opportunity with a large pipeline.
2. Establish and strengthen rapport.
3. Ask for permission and stick to your time.
4. Ask open-ended questions to determine the customer's objectives and values.
5. Solve the customer's problem in light of their risks and opportunities.
6. Ask for the business.
7. Negotiate post-close items.

That seventh step is the concept of negotiating in good faith with the intention of creating value for both parties. Here are some ideas on how this connects to customer success.

Negotiate with value

Once the deal is cut, there are typically numerous things to negotiate. Often this can be divisive: you try to get the other party to retreat or disqualify their views. The "value" is fixed. Someone wins; someone loses—and the loser usually plans for retaliation.

The customer success approach to negotiations is to expand the pie. The "value" is flexible and can be broadened. The customer success approach views the relationship as a long-term one. The goal is to collaborate. Open communication is the primary tool here. Both, or all, parties plan for reward and renewed contracts.

The process of value negotiation includes a commitment to delve into enough detail with your new customer to find ways you can both come out ahead (see Appendix B for more information). If done properly, no customer feels gouged. And you are always paid at least a reasonable profit margin. We don't accept loss leaders.

"The process of value negotiation includes a commitment to delve into enough detail with your new customer to find ways you can both come out ahead."

The benefit of this approach is twofold. First, you are always able to finish the project because you charged enough to make a profit. Second, by not gouging even when you could, the small amount of money you may have left on the table is more than offset with repeat business and access to bigger contracts in the future.

So, what is the process?

1. **Set fair rules up front.** Establish time limits for a final decision and approval process. Get agreement on how disagreements will be handled.

2. **Stay honest and open.** Reveal company strengths and weaknesses. Listen to genuine needs and concerns and fears.

3. **Be collaborative.** Attempt to problem-solve together. Lay out the variables of terms, price, timing, and breadth of solution while discussing with each other the relative weight of each variable. Seek opportunities that are of high value to your new customer that don't cost you that much to deliver.

4. **Separate people from the problem.** Don't get preoccupied with your own position. Put yourself (and your company) in the other party's place, then make proposals that will appeal to both sides. Seek value for your customer.

5. **Focus on interests, not on positions.** Interests are basic human needs such as security, economic well-being, a win for the company, etc. Speak clearly about your own interests and listen to and acknowledge the interests of the other party.

6. **Use creative problem-solving.** There are a lot of ways to solve problems. And, lots of ways to trade value. If you're not tied emotionally to the one way you want to do something, you may uncover an even better value for your company.

Using that approach to negotiations produces a fair and collaborative way to contract negotiations and sets the stage for repeat business, particularly on large complex projects.

The business developer is essential to customer success. She can set the expectation at or below what your company can deliver, and she can negotiate a good margin. The customer will be delighted when you meet or exceed his expectations, and you will be rewarded with repeat business and enthusiastic referrals. That is *customer loyalty*—and that increases the value of your company.

The business developer can really help your company. Please see Appendix E for what we have learned about behaviors that predict success for this critical position.

***

Set the stage for your operations team to provide exceptional customer success by having a well-trained sales team to *Go Ahead* and establish the customer expectation at or below your ability to deliver the product or services. To pull this off:

1. Sell with integrity.
2. Negotiate with value.

Chapter 9: Customer Success Training

"The first thing any man has to know is how to handle himself. Training counts. You can't win any game unless you are ready to win." —Connie Mack

Winning in the marketplace is not a contest of gathering the most information. We have plenty of data. We know enough. It is about implementing what we know. So, train your people to confidently focus on making the customer successful. Here are seven training tips.

1. Simplify the rules and policies.

Often company policies or work rules result in poor customer service delivery. How often do your customer service representatives say, "We are not allowed to . . . I'm sorry, sir, that is against company policy . . ."? They may as well say, "I am sorry, sir, my company doesn't trust me to think this one through, so I am going to have to make it hard on you."

Usually, company rules and policies are crafted with good intentions. You need policies for timely payment, contract terms, etc. But do you need as many as you have established? Certain rules can aggravate a good customer, cause employees to look foolish, and ultimately embarrass the company.

They may as well say, "I am sorry, sir, my company doesn't trust me to think this one through, so I am going to have to make it hard on you."

Sometimes a rule results from being burned. One customer doesn't pay on a timely basis, so payment terms are tightened for *all* customers. Now, all those perfectly reliable customers are irritated. A much better solution is to train your employees to be innovative in their solutions and relax the rules. Teach them how to spot a credit risk. Armed with the right principles and concepts, they can intelligently manage a variety of customer situations. They are equipped to *Go Ahead* and handle the issue with common sense and proper analysis.

When you rely on rules, you often make customer-related decisions based on the rules rather than the customer's needs. Think about how this works. Your employees are applying their energy and talent toward obeying the rule instead of helping the customer succeed. This is a corporate disease I call "rule myopia."

And, rule myopia injects an attitude. Ultimately, the customer of a business infected with rule myopia ends up doing all the work to be served. As the customer, we've all engaged in work-arounds to combat rule myopia.

"And, rule myopia injects an attitude. Ultimately, the customer of a business infected with rule myopia ends up doing all the work to get served."

Consider the restaurant setting, where we must be humble and diligent to make sure the waitress doesn't mess up our order—she is a perfectly wonderful person, but she isn't good at memorizing things. She is following a rule to never write anything down. But no customer is impressed with that rule when the medium rare order comes out well done. So, we as the customer become proactive! We have no choice. We like the food, but we must be a good customer to survive the bad service that results from the rules.

Instead, encourage customer success representatives to shift their focus away from rigid adherence to rules so they can solve the customer's problem. Encourage them to *Go Ahead* and make the best decision they can to serve the customer profitably. In an environment of freedom within the boundaries of proper principles, common sense flourishes.

The primary tone of the work environment should be trust and empowerment. You can't establish work rules that cover every scenario anyway. The better tool is to give them the responsibility and authority they need to handle situations intelligently. And tell them to *Go Ahead*!

"The primary tone of the work environment should be trust and empowerment. You can't establish work rules that cover every scenario anyway."

2. Create consultants not technicians.

If you have technicians or service representatives, consider beefing up the job title to sound more like a consultant or engineer. With a little training they can be equipped to go beyond the limits of a traditional service representative. They are empowered to make great decisions and function as consultants.

Have three goals for them as consultants:

1. Deliver service so exceptional that the customer is more successful with you than without you.
2. Continually educate the customer on the numerous support services you provide.
3. Cause the customer to understand and genuinely believe that the service fee is inconsequential compared to the added value you provide.

3. Train employees with phone skills.

Since many prefer digital communications, often people are not very good on the phone. Here is where you can set yourself apart as a company: train your people on good old-fashioned phone skills.

- **Answer in person.** The first voice a customer hears should be a live human, not a recorded one, whenever possible. I wonder how many frustrated customers hang up halfway through the maze of automated options. And how many of those complaints are a potential gold mine of information that could help protect your company from disruption. Consider bucking the trend and front-loading with real people.
- **Put people first.** A keyboard pounding in the background can be frustrating for the customer. Make the equivalent of eye contact over the phone, which is an immediate focused conversation, acknowledging the importance of the customer.
- **Use courtesy and kindness.** Always be cordial. Never say to a customer, "I'm really busy." You are never too busy to give the customer your full attention. Always make the customer feel good that he called you.
- **Employ energetic listening.** Take focused time with your callers. Edgy, abrupt answers convey a lack of care. Do not engage in other activities outside the

conversation you are having with the caller. Never eat or chew gum while on the phone.

- **Use clear vocabulary.** Speak on the customer's level. Jargon is confusing to callers and makes them feel inferior. Use plain English. Think about what you are saying before you say it. Articulate clearly and professionally.

- **Practice blind friendliness.** Be friendly even before you know to whom you are talking. Answer the phone with a smile. Your tone of voice should always be upbeat. The person on the other end of that line could be the most important customer in the company's history.

- **Use common pleasantries.** Everyone used to say "thank you" and "you're welcome." Now, it is common to abbreviate everything. Customers appreciate the more formal expressions.

- **Convey availability to all customers.** "He is in a meeting. Is this a matter you feel is of an urgent enough nature that I should interrupt? Is it acceptable to have him call you back as soon as he is finished? Can someone else be of assistance?" It should not be the customer's job to ask these questions.

- **Avoid backroom descriptions.** Customers are not interested in the mechanics of the business. Provide covered explanations. They are interested in their problem being fixed, not how your copy machine sorts and staples.

122

- **Always close the loop.** If you are patching a call through to someone else, go the extra mile to make sure the customer is properly connected. If you promise to deliver a message, make sure it is delivered.

"Practice blind friendliness. Be friendly even before you know to whom you are talking."

4. Promote empathy.

An effective but often missed concept is empathy. Empathy is expressing genuine concern for the plight of another. When you really listen to what the customer is saying, you know what they need and expect. When you don't take the time to listen, you are just stabbing in the dark.

"When you really listen to what the customer is saying, you know what they need and expect. When you don't take the time to listen, you are just stabbing in the dark."

Here is a simple way to reinforce this concept. The net promoter score (NPS) has been very helpful in quantifying customer loyalty, but at the end of the day, we still train our team to understand the big picture questions so we don't lose sight of the emotional connection.

- **How do you know what the customer wants?** Ask her. "What would a satisfactory result look like?"
- **How do you know what the customer means?** Ask him. "You say you want your work environment to be 'nicer.' Could you kindly clarify that for me? What is an example of how it is not that way now?"
- **How do you know when you are helping the customer become more successful?** Know their environment. Visit their location and observe their culture, or ask about it over the phone. Expect their point of view to be different from yours. Find out their frame of reference, their context. Ask the customer, "You know what services we render. If you could wave a magic wand, what role would you like for me to play in your business?"

5. Handle irate customers with empathy and solutions.

Regardless of how exceptional your products or services are, you will still encounter irate customers. Even if you are perfect in every way, you have customers that will be irrational. The general level of courtesy and formality in our culture has declined—social scientists point to the impact of social media and a host of social ills that have resulted in a less civil code of conduct. As a result, more people than even a decade ago think they have a right to be abusive when things don't go the way they want. And, that spews out on the company's customer service representative. So, in our training, we endeavor to help separate the issue from the person with these eight steps.

1. **Expect irrational customers.** The paragraph above can be amplified to help the customer success representative anticipate that not everyone will be filled with decorum. And the customer has the potential to be an "A+" customer. So treat all customers with respect and honor. Even if the company later decides to cancel the customer, treat them well during this interaction.

2. **Respond to their problem as if it were your own.** Start with empathy. The first thing you should think is, *"If I were in their shoes, I might feel the same way."*

3. **Do not apologize insincerely for something that is not your fault.** That is a customer service technique. Since it is not genuine, it isn't sustainable. You can still empathize. The first point to get across is some rendition of "If I were in your situation, I may be just as upset." This often gets the customer to realize they are coming across angry. In some cases, that alone will calm them down.

4. **Ask the customer's permission to solve their real problem.** Refrain from immediately solving the problem. If they are irate, they will not hear what you have to say anyway. Attempt to get an acknowledgment that it is acceptable to proceed.

The second thing you say is, "May I work with you to resolve this issue?" or "I would like to solve this problem, and I think I can. May I ask you a couple of questions?"

5. **Solve the problem.** Follow the process outlined in the problem-solving schematic in the next section. In many instances it can be abbreviated, but follow a process—the customer will feel served and that you are utilizing a checklist for his benefit.

6. **Provide closure during the call.** Sometimes you cannot solve the problem immediately. In this case you say, "I will call you back in thirty minutes with the answer. Will that be acceptable?" If you have solved the problem, simply finish with, "Is the solution we just worked through satisfactory?"

7. **Close the loop.** Always follow up. If the problem was not solved and you said you would call back in thirty minutes, call back in thirty minutes. If you solved the problem and they said the solution was fine, then give them one last opportunity to prove that they are now OK. "I appreciated the opportunity to work with you on this solution, and I am genuinely glad you called. Is there anything else I can help you with?"

8. **Respond to the customer even when you don't want to.** We all have customers that make us uptight. In a brief offline, for-internal-ears-only meeting, spend five to ten minutes venting. Discuss

the real reasons you do not want to interact with the mean customer. You do not like his disposition. You are afraid to explain the error you made. You think he is too much of a bully. Maybe he always has a complaint, tries to renegotiate the fees, or just has an obnoxious personality. After you vent, your time is up. Call him now, not later. You will find out what is wrong and have the potential to resolve the issue.

"Close the loop. Always follow up."

6. Teach your people to analyze so they can solve problems.

When you train your people how to analyze, they will be able to solve most any problem. Create a thinking environment. Your product or service might be copied by the competition, but make it hard for them to copy your customer success methodology. Using a problem-solving schematic will set you apart. In addition, it broadens the job for your employees. They gain confidence by knowing how to think in a disciplined manner and guide a customer through an intelligent process. This is the schematic we use—feel free to customize it to your situation:

- **Define the problem.** Usually, we attempt to go straight to fixing what we *think* the problem is based on past experiences. That can be dangerous. Take a minute to regroup. Be careful not to allow the stress of the dilemma to outweigh the actual problem at hand. Establish the boundaries of the problem with questions. When did this problem start? How big is this problem? Who are the key players? What is the actual problem? Why is this a problem? Why did this become a problem?

- **Test the other side of the issue to help properly define the problem.** Ask questions as the advocate from more than one perspective. Break down the problem into its components. What are the risks? Is there a public relations issue? How would other employees view this? Does this adversely impact our vendors?

- **Evaluate alternative solutions.** There is rarely only one way to solve a problem. Endeavor to find at least two solutions. We want them to compete. Even if you think the first solution is clearly the best, oblige yourself to push past your bias and consider both solutions equally.

- **Critique the alternatives.** Weigh the pros and cons of each alternative. If complex, numerically rank the various columns and rows of issues. Think in reverse. At this stage, you likely have a clear and articulate understanding of the problem and the possible solutions.

- **Select the best alternative.** This solution should feel solid. You should be able to move forward with confidence. Usually a risk is associated with every business decision. That's business. But with this process, you will mitigate some of that risk. Now, the decision is yours, and you have full authority and responsibility to make the best decision you can. You most likely have made the best choice. Select it and don't look back.

- **Implement the solution.** There are usually two or three viable solutions for most problems. That is why we say don't look back after you have selected what you believe is the best alternative. Nothing should get in the way of execution. Execution is everything. If it is complex, put an implementation plan together and execute with precision. If it is simple, just *Go Ahead* and get it done.

"Execution is everything. If it is complex, put an implementation plan together and execute with precision. If it is simple, just Go Ahead and get it done."

7. Explain the reasons behind your approach.

Sometimes, companies train employees without explaining the why. The concept of customer success often solicits endorsement on its own merits, but you gain an additional edge when you give your employees the following reasons for implementing a customer success approach:

- **It is always less expensive to do the job right the first time.** If you make a mistake, the company may have to pay a credit or offer a refund. If you create an error, you have to fix the problem and make it right, while concurrently handling other customers' inquiries. This increases the odds of making yet another mistake, starting a vicious cycle.

- **People are screaming for a genuine touch.** The world is more automated than ever. Encounters with people are more important than ever. Humans need a human touch. Offset our high-tech culture with a high-touch encounter.

- **Customers are willing to pay more for the company's products and services when they are accompanied by exceptional service.**

- **Delighted customers are likely to be repeat buyers,** because they are more concerned about their time than ever. They prefer not to shop around. If properly served, they won't need to. When a customer purchases from you again without comparison shopping, it dramatically lowers the company's sales and marketing costs.

- **Thrilled customers will share good news with their friends.** When the customer success approach is taking hold, the customer will trust you with your quality products and services. Their trust translates into a willingness to use their reputation on your behalf. A referral is worth a lot. Think of every service call with that customer's best referral in mind.

- **Customers are not an interruption to our day.** They are the primary purpose of our day—they are the reason our job exists. You can get so busy working on this project or that report that you forget the reason we are in business. Customers butter our bread.

"Customers are not an interruption to our day. They are the primary purpose of our day—they are the reason our job exists."

***

Keys to customer success training:

1. Simplify the rules and policies.
2. Create consultants not technicians.
3. Train employees with phone skills.
4. Promote empathy.
5. Handle irate customers with empathy and solutions.
6. Teach your people to analyze so they can solve problems.
7. Explain the reasons behind your approach.

Chapter 10: Keeping the Momentum

"Spend a lot of time talking to customers face-to-face. You'd be amazed how many companies don't listen to their customers." —Ross Perot

When Benjamin Franklin started his publishing business in Philadelphia, he had no money and was relatively unknown. He had just fled his abusive big brother's print shop in Boston. Now he was competing with a wealthy, famous publisher.

When Franklin began printing his little newspaper, the big competitor decided he would slash his prices and drive Franklin out of business. How could Franklin possibly succeed against such odds? Innovative Benjamin did it by providing information that people wanted to read.

He persistently asked his customers the right questions. "You have seen my paper; what would you do to make it better?" He'd say, "Here's the leading paper. It costs you four cents. But would you pay five cents for a paper that had information you want?"

Benjamin Franklin listened to his customers, kept listening to them, and delivered. He responded to the customers' wishes based on his superior expertise and, as a result, became extraordinarily wealthy.

"Benjamin Franklin listened to his customers, kept listening to them, and delivered. He responded to the customers' wishes based on his superior expertise and, as a result, became extraordinarily wealthy."

Customer success is a superior corporate strategy. It doesn't force the customer into a box. It finds out what the customer wants and takes it further.

Keep the momentum:

> 1. Listen to your customers.
> 2. Keep listening to them.
> 3. Deliver.

Go, CEO!

If you are the CEO, customer success plays a role in simplifying and clarifying your challenging job. You have two primary audiences and four responsibilities.

First, you serve your external stakeholders. And, to your external stakeholders you have two primary responsibilities:

1. You are the investor. This topic is outside the scope of this book, but your investors invested in your business (and even if that is just you, you should still separate the roles in your mind); you deploy capital to increase value. You are "el jefe" of capital allocation strategy, and that is your external lever to increase long-term business value. For me, that includes driving the company's capital allocation objectives of improving free cash flow and investing in projects and acquisitions with likely returns above the cost of equity and debt. That factors in the hurdle of reasonable estimations of market risk.

2. You are the customer loyalty strategist. Your COO will pull it off, but you set the strategy. If you don't have a good customer experience strategy that you like, consider the five steps outlined in my book *The Magic Wand*, provided in summary form in Appendix A.

Second, you serve your internal stakeholders. And, to your internal stakeholders you have two primary responsibilities:

1. You build an exceptional company culture. Use some rendition of the three cultural pillars of Integrity, Innovation, and Invitation. This helps create an

environment that enables your team to recruit and retain world-class talent. To do that with people who possess integrity, you'll benefit from championing the customer success mindset.

2. You align your team to increase business value. This includes establishing the strategy for a map of all touchpoints that crystalizes every team member's OKRs (objectives and key results or whatever metric you prefer). This helps your team align with where you want them to go so they can help you increase business value. Your busy COO and other executives will pull this off, but you are charged with the strategy. The customer success mindset, coupled with the second and third steps found in *The Magic Wand*, will separate you from the competition here (see Appendix A).

Go Ahead!

Build your business on principles, do what you say you're going to do when you say you're going to do it, provide an encouraging, uplifting environment where your people are motivated to innovate, create an invitational atmosphere—a drama-free, collaborative, high-energy environment that motivates your team to jump out of bed and come to work, is a magnet for top talent, and is a draw for new customers— and champion the customer success mindset.

I know there's a lot of discussion about AI (artificial intelligence) these days, and while it can provide you with actionable market intelligence, computers can only do so much. Humans are made in the image of God. Humans can feel and understand the story of the emotional connection with your product or service. They can help provide you with market intelligence that will not only equip you to mitigate against a competitor but position you to be the disrupter. They can help you give customers what they want before they ask!

So, *Go Ahead*! Unleash a contagious customer success culture.

"They can help provide you with actionable market intelligence that will not only equip you to mitigate against a competitor but position you to be the disrupter. They can help you give customers what they want before they ask!"

Appendixes

Appendix A: The Five Secrets of Exceptional CX

The Five Secrets of Exceptional CX (customer experience)

1. Develop and deploy an objective, measurable CX vision—ask empowering questions.
2. Understand each step and touchpoint in the customer's path and how the customer feels about it—ask empowering questions.
3. Reorganize all customer touchpoints to create a better, more real-time dialogue with them that solicits from them the kind of interactions that deepen loyalty—ask empowering questions.
4. Recognize and reward CX knowledge throughout the company—ask empowering questions.
5. Communicate and measure CX everywhere—from top to bottom—ask empowering questions.

A good question is empowering. The idea of the Magic Wand Question is that it is designed to provide the customer with the emotional context of influential power.

It is an empowering question with an open-ended design and the intent to solicit an open-ended answer. An open-ended answer does not have too many preconceived ideas. There are, of course, natural business constraints, but beyond those reasonable limitations, an open-ended answer comes with the belief that it carries weight. It will often provide outside-the-box ideas.

If the company can profitably implement ideas from the open-ended answer, this is a golden opportunity to execute an improved service delivery in which the customer has some ownership. If the company executes upon the improved solution, the value proposition is better, the overall enjoyment of the product or service improves, and the customer's loyalty to your Brand is the happy result.

With the employees and leaders and customers participating in improved service delivery, it provides the company with a transcendent purpose. It is fun to deliver what we know the customer prefers versus some guess of what we think they want.

And that yields a great customer experience.

The Five Secrets is an appendix from the book, The Magic Wand: Creating an Exceptional Customer Experience, By Barry Farah 2017

Appendix B: Sales and Negotiations IBM Sales Approach

(This is paraphrased from my perspective and is not intended to be an exact replica of what IBM would authorize, but they deserve credit for pioneering the concepts.)

The four components of IBM direct sales:

1. Build Rapport
   - Research the company and individuals
   - Meet them with a smile
   - Identify their preferred style and then adapt to it
   - Watch your time

2. Understand Customer Objectives
   - Business environment and initiatives
   - IT environment and technology preferences
   - Pain chain, key players, budget, time frame
   - Conditions for satisfaction
   - Develop and confirm plans that link to business initiatives
   - Establish buying vision with the customer
   - Establish power sponsor access
   - Restate objectives and gain confirmation

3. Explain the Customer Solution with Your Products and Services
   - Articulate your capabilities
   - Evaluate alternative solutions
   - Agree to move forward with preliminary solution
   - Develop solution with customer
   - Define value proposition criteria
   - Restate objectives with agreement
   - Present solution to their objectives only
   - Obtain objective feedback

4. Close
   - Value negotiate
   - Resolve concerns
   - Ask, "Is there any way our proposed solution does not support your objectives?"
   - Ask, "Can we move toward a statement of work this week?"
   - Sign agreement
   - Implement solution
   - Measure the benefits
   - Gain customer's acknowledgment of value of solution

Sandler Sales Approach

(This is paraphrased from my perspective and is not intended to be an exact replica of what Sandler would authorize, but they deserve credit for pioneering the concepts.)

1. **Build and Sustain a Relationship**
   - Rapport (Connect)
   - Sincerity to help the customer solve problems or face challenges or achieve goals (Communicate)

- Control the selling process (Control)
- Establish up-front agreements on each element of the process
- Determine who will be responsible for each element

2. **Qualify the Opportunity**
   - Focus on degree of fit (Pain)
   - Your capabilities
   - Your problem or challenge or goal
   - Determine if prospect is willing to commit necessary resources (Budget)
   - Determine the way your offer will be judged (Decision)
   - Who will judge your offer? Will they be at the presentation?
   - How will it be judged? What are the criteria for success?

3. **Close the Sale**
   - Restate solution (Objectives)
   - Include only qualified prospects in the closing phase
   - They have previously agreed to make a decision at the conclusion of a presentation
   - Presentation should only focus on the pain uncovered (Fulfillment)
   - Post-Sell activities "lock up" the sale and facilitate a transition from Buyer and Seller to Partners working together to solve a problem or achieve a goal (Post-sell)
   - Obtain a yes, no, or "let's move to the next step"

Value Negotiations

Value negotiations—whether with a customer, another vendor, or your employees—treat the other party respectfully with the mindset that we may likely be negotiating something in the future. As a result, create value to offer the potential for a win-win scenario for each party. Wise agreement is agreement that meets the interests of both parties to the extent possible, is long lasting, and keeps the door open for the next negotiation.

Steps for any value negotiation

1. Ask questions to discover the benefits and top values
   - For the other party
   - For you

2. Prepare for the negotiation
   - Choose the goal
   - Understand the parties
   - Detail out the truth
   - Think through risks
   - Rehearse the value
   - Role-play a challenging situation

3. Address the three elements of negotiation
   - Content
   - Process to achieve outcome
   - Relationships of all involved

4. Get to a yes
   - Separate people from the problem
   - Focus on interests not positions
   - Invent options for mutual gain
   - Insist on using objective criteria

Maximize value in any negotiation

- Maximize rapport.
- Build trust.
- Develop understanding.
- Know their value proposition.
- Reaffirm your agreement.
- Deepen your commitment.
- Drive for satisfaction.
- Build a lasting relationship.
- Enjoy the relationship.

Appendix C: Otto's Auto Repair Shop

Auto repair at Otto's

How do you implement the customer success strategy in a retail environment? Well, let's pick one of the most competitive retail industries: the auto repair shop. This is a tough business. When a customer comes to you, it is because something isn't working right.

Unfortunately, scam artists have tarnished the industry. Since customers have heard these horror stories, they come to you with suspicion in their eyes. To compound your problem, there are gazillions of honest competitors. So it is not as simple as waving a banner and saying, "We're the good guys, honest."

Here's how customer success–minded Otto's auto repair shop would be run.

First, Otto's would have an extremely clean facility. The cleanest part of the facility would be the inviting waiting area. There would be a nice place for kids to play and read books with a rubber-padded floor and walls. That room would have semi-soundproof glass. Want to listen to your kids? Simply plug in the headphones at the port in one of the chairs and turn to channel 1.

Would you prefer not to listen to your kids? Would you rather listen to classical music and read an old book not available online? Fine, get the book off the shelf and turn to channel 2. Or kick back on the recliner chair, watch your own show on your own medium, and enjoy your time.

The layout of the shop would not require you to wade through a pile of tires to get to the customer service counter. When you walk in, a well-groomed and knowledgeable employee at the circular customer success booth greets you. After you explain your car problem, he says, "We will handle everything, Mr. Jones. Allow me to escort you to the waiting area."

He explains the complimentary coffee and tea station; the honor system for the low-cost snack area (including fresh and healthy options); the Wi-Fi access; the variety of reading materials; the audio system for music, podcasts, and the play area; and in which lane to look for your car. Finally, he puts you at ease. "I hope you enjoy your stay, but we will endeavor to get you on your way as soon as possible. A transportation repair specialist will come to you in a few minutes with a diagnosis of your automobile's problems. We will then describe how long it will take for us to fix the problem. If that doesn't work for you, we will provide a Lyft back to your home or office."

This employee took an additional four minutes with you. And he wins you as a customer for a long time.

You smell fresh-brewed coffee and freshly baked cinnamon rolls. (Otto's wants you to smell cinnamon, not grease.) The waiting area is exceptionally comfortable and strategically located between the play area and the workshop. This adult area has access to a small library of current trade journals and great works of literature. Or you can hook up your digital device to one of the outlets at the desk area and access your email or finish up a work project. The library, trade journal subscriptions, beverages, and Wi-Fi might only cost a few thousand dollars, but the shop would more than make that up in lower marketing costs. Otto's wants you to enjoy waiting—you should be almost disappointed when the car is fixed so soon!

Otto's would hire the best mechanics in town. They would know how to diagnose problems accurately, and they would be the best at fixing them. Otto's is trying to impress both the customer and the mechanic. They have exceptionally high standards.

The mechanics would wear sharp-looking uniforms. The company logo would be on the front of each employee's shirt and a snappy customer success motto would be neatly placed on the back. The owner wants each customer and employee to see that motto. All the employees would have their hair nicely trimmed. They would all go through a half-day customer success charm school. "Yes, ma'am; yes, sir; please and thank you" would be required work rules. (Yes, that is legal.)

It does not matter if there is a shortage of mechanics. Pay is important, and these would be among the highest-paid mechanics in town. But what is really attracting them and keeping them is their pride in participating in Otto's corporate success. They are part of the "elite."

With soundproof glass separating the waiting room from the repair area, a customer could easily see his car and the employees would know they are always being watched, but not heard, by the customer. They would not be permitted to swear, but they would be encouraged to shout clean jokes or sing off-key to the music. The customer who is looking in would see a lot of fast-working, energetic, clean-cut mechanics with big smiles.

The result? Getting your car repaired was less painful than you expected—enjoyable, in fact. You won't mind coming back. Otto's didn't just fix your car, but your kids were entertained, you enjoyed a satisfying snack, took care of work or personal business, and read or listened to something that made you a richer person— all while waiting!

As the customer success employee graciously explains your invoice, you find that they did not just adjust your brakes, but they have secured that your transportation will be safe. You reluctantly leave the shop to get into your car—and it's spotless! Your seat and

151

mirrors are returned to their original positions. And the radio is not blaring. You find a little mint on the dash attached to a handwritten note: "Thanks for coming in! We wish you safe and pleasant travels."

Customers would be willing to pay for this level of service—and they'd tell their friends.

Appendix D: Integrity, Innovation, and Invitation

Integrity

We do what we say we're going to do when we say we are going to do it, even when you are not watching, providing you with solutions that are whole and complete.

- Closes the loop effectively and regularly
- Maintains a Customer Success Mindset through challenges
- Serves customers proactively (as opposed to mere reactive service)
- Seeks to discover and understand the customer's values and history
- Conveys humility and diligence
- Communicates effectively
- Takes ownership of outcome goals
- Regularly displays energetic listening skills
- Avoids giving customers "backroom" details
- Handles irate customers with skill and purpose

Innovation

With intellectual curiosity, we dig deeper and often uncover the best solutions after the project has commenced, delivering to you exceptional quality and unexpected value on budget.

- Embraces a spirit of enterprise (driven to succeed) in all we do
- Anticipates real needs
- Focuses on the root cause
- Employs the "backflip" mindset for the customer at the appropriate time
- Leads the customer with expertise when appropriate
- Demonstrates an ability to be quick and agile
- Employs good telephone savvy and conveys empathy to the customer
- Fixes corporate bottlenecks
- Energetically gives one's best to the team each day
- Owns the problem-solving schematic and consistently implements and leads with it in dealing with both internal and external customers

Invitation

We create an inviting, collaborative, and drama-free work environment that motivates our employees to jump out of bed to come to work, is a magnet for top talent, and draws new clients to some of the best services they will ever experience.

- Helps keep negative politics at bay
- Diligently works to resolve conflict in the workplace
- Practices harmonious employee relations
- Able to share the vision, mission, and values

- Is an effective communicator:
- Know your goal
- Understand your receiver
- Utilize the appropriate mode
- Measure the impact feedback
- Conveys availability with both internal and external customers
- Conveys selling philosophy values

Maintenance of Values

Build exercises off the customer experience vision statement to ingrain the concept and values into the everyday work environment and to reinforce the customer success culture. Below are the primary reminders that we use to ensure we are practicing what we are preaching on the values of integrity, innovation, and invitation:

- Customer satisfaction requires an entrepreneurial backflip.
- Integrity is not to be compromised: be honest, fair, consistent.
- Commitments made must be fulfilled.
- Never cut corners; get the details right the first time. Care about the solution.
- Be humble—don't dominate, don't judge, don't gossip.
- Do unto others as you would have them do unto you.
- I own the mistake, but we fix it together.
- We share the glory, but I excel individually.

Appendix E: Behaviors of a Salesperson

Assertive/Initiator: Is the person a doer? Does he attempt to solve problems without a lot of prodding? Or is he a procrastinator? I'm looking for aggressive, strong responses that are genuine.

Persuasive/Convincer: Can the person persuade a prospect? Customer? Employee? We'll say, "Here, take this pencil and sell it to me." I'm looking for the establishment of a need, not just the features and benefits. I'm also looking to see if she can close. Can this person change my mind? Can this person develop a need for something I didn't know I needed?

Values/Integrity: Is the person honest and trustworthy? What is his response to white lies? Have his ethics been put to the test in a situation in the past? How does he respond to questions about integrity?

Empathy/Relationship Skills: Does the person get along with others, and can she build long-term relationships? Does she know how to genuinely say, "I know how you feel"? We ask open-ended questions that touch on emotional intelligences skills.

Ego Strength/Conqueror: Does the person have a killer instinct? Is he tenacious? Can he get up when knocked down? Is he absolutely committed to winning? Five other salespeople may be in the lobby. Exceptional salespeople love the hunt and the thrill of winning a sale, especially when they do not offer the lowest price. The service offering at our company has incredible value, but it is largely intangible. It requires the ability to look the prospect in the eye and challenge him.

Motivated/Driver: Why do you want a career with us in sales? Money should be a part of this answer. A big talker likes to get out and talk to people. Not on our nickel. A good salesperson likes to get out and listen to people and properly determine if a business relationship is feasible—quickly. I'm looking to see if she is willing to subordinate her ability to make a great presentation for the benefit of closing the deal. Can she ask difficult questions, even if personally uncomfortable with the question? That shows motivation.

Personal Ambition: If the candidate's motivation is to be a general manager, then I'm not sure I like what I'm hearing for this position. I want a clearly thought-out, mature, honest self-assessment. Does this candidate know his strengths and weaknesses? The best candidate knows he can sell and knows he would make a lousy manager.

Appendix F: New Hire Orientation

Congratulations, you have hired an excellent partner-in-training or at least a great associate! Now you have a golden opportunity to make an excellent first impression.

First, go over your values. Our companies use an info graphic that helps explain integrity, innovation, and invitation. There should be some sense of excitement here, because during the interview process you would have discussed these values in detail and the new employee should have already convinced you that she agrees. You can also go over your mission and vision, but I encourage values first. Those never change.

Before you have your new associate fill out a bunch of forms, introduce her to everyone in the office. Assume that she will make significant contributions to the future success of your company, and treat her that way. When you introduce her, make it short but cover the qualifications. "This is Jane. She brings enviable educational attainments and work experiences. We think she will fit in well with our culture and provide significant assistance where it is needed. Please make her feel welcome and answer any questions she may have."

After introductions, spend some time explaining what will happen over the balance of the day. "Your main goal today is to get acclimated. We also want you to thoroughly understand our culture and our philosophy because we want you to help us preserve it."

Next, take the employee to her desk with the basic employment forms. After she completes the forms, go over the employee handbook and have her sign the acknowledgment form. Explain the health plans, the 401(k) retirement plan, and any other pension or profit sharing plans. Give the employee time to digest this information. Attempt to answer all her questions on benefits issues during the first day.

Now, rehash the values. For our employees, that is integrity, innovation, and invitation. Ask her if she has any questions. In a low-key manner, ask her to restate them to you in her own words. Then, tell her how important it is to you for her to help refresh everyone on the value of the values.

Let the new employee look over the shoulder of another associate for an hour or so before you take her out to lunch. Over lunch find out about her family life, her favorite hobbies, etc. Be respectful and laid back. This should not feel like an interview. Convey genuine interest in your new associate, not just what she can do for you. After lunch, let her interact with some other employees for an hour or so back at the office.

Getting around the office

Almost any employee can administer an overview training of the business in less than twenty minutes, yet businesses often overlook it. This can be embarrassing for everyone.

Once, I called a prestigious law firm that served one of my businesses. They had offices all over the country. I needed their assistance in another state. Not only did the new employee not know whether they had an office in this other location, but she also thought they only had one office. I had to persuade her that her firm was national and guide her through the process of helping me.

Do your new employees know where all of your offices are located? Do they know what products and services you sell? Do

160

they know your processes? Do they know your hours of business? Do they know how to use the phone? Train new employees in company logistics early on. Isn't this obvious? Well, even the most respected companies can oops on this one.

I met a gentleman on an airplane who told me a humorous story that illustrates the importance of this training. He had called Microsoft to get some customer assistance. He must have been connected to a brand spanking new employee. He asked for some help with Windows. The employee replied with confidence, "Sir, we are not a hardware store; we only sell software."

CPSIA information can be obtained
at www.ICGtesting.com
Printed in the USA
BVHW040421200719
553751BV00011B/23/P